T0273132

SURF, SWEAT AND TEARS

SURF, SWEAT AND TEARS

The Epic Life and Mysterious Death of
Edward George William Omar Deerhurst

Andy Martin

OR Books
New York · London

For Duncan Coventry and Young Ted

All rights information: rights@orbooks.com
Visit our website at www.orbooks.com
First printing 2020

Published by OR Books, New York and London

Library of Congress Cataloging-in-Publication Data: A catalog record for this book is available from the Library of Congress.

Typeset by Lapiz Digital Services.

paperback ISBN 978-1-68219-231-3 • ebook ISBN 978-1-68219-233-7

"The ideal of sliding is therefore a sliding that does not leave any trace: that is, sliding on water."

Jean-Paul Sartre, *Being and Nothingness*

1.

This is how Rabbit thought Ted had died:

It was one of those fall days with a foretaste of the winter to come. A big day at Sunset. Obviously Ted had to go for it even if he knew he shouldn't. And he deserved respect for that. If he really was in as bad shape as they said he was, then he was a hero every time he paddled out. He could die at any moment in the water.

The pre-winter swell sparked off breaks all along the North Shore, but none more so than Sunset. Sunset was known for hoovering up every passing swell, something to do with the configuration of the reef. A storm way up in the Aleutians thousands of miles away and now, in the middle of the Pacific, the same pulse was cranking out perfect waves, almost like a machine. Of course there was no such thing as a perfect wave, there was only ever the wave that was in front of you, and if you surfed it then it was about as close to perfection as you were ever liable to get. On this particular day, Sunset was like an enthusiastic young dog you threw a stick for, jumping and leaping way up in the air, off the leash, running free, bounding up and down for sheer joy. But, by the same token, unpredictable, erratic, out of control.

And Ted was part of it. He was always part of it. He was a little bit like that young dog. Or a flying fish, glinting silver in the sun. He thought of Sunset as his wave now. And he couldn't not turn up on a big day. Especially this early in the season. It would be a dereliction of duty. He would be like a deserter, chickening out under fire. Ted would never chicken out. The more anybody told him to go back and retreat, the more he would go forwards and push on even unto death. That was his way. He had, after all, only just turned forty. He wasn't dead yet. So he paddled out. He would always paddle out, come what may. That was the thing about Sunset, it almost sucked you out regardless. The rip was like a conveyor belt, carrying you out into the great maw of the wave, all you had to do was hop on. A few effortless strokes and you were right out there, way out the back, beyond the impact zone, where all these superb unbroken waves stacked up like planes over an airport waiting to descend. All you had to do was select which one you wanted to ride. Sunset had the feeling of inevitability.

Maybe it appealed to Ted's sense of history. In a way, this was about as primitive as you could get. As long as there had been oceans and islands, waves like these ones had slammed up against the shore. The ancient Hawaiians had surfed these very same waves–centuries before Captain Cook ever set sail, in the golden age before evangelical Puritans persuaded them to put some clothes on–and Ted was only carrying on an immemorial tradition. He really felt that. Like an Olympic athlete taking firm possession of a baton, passed on from one man to another, for ever and ever. A gentle offshore breeze pinned the waves back and groomed them neatly and held the door open long enough, just for you, almost like the elevator in a classy hotel, so you had time to get in properly before dropping down the face.

The set of the day manifested itself on the horizon. Wave after wave reared up out of the blue like humpback whales breaching. Not too many guys out on this glorious morning. Ted had the rare feeling that it was just him out here and the ocean. He could take his pick, like pulling a card out of a whole pack that a conjuror had fanned out in front of him. And lo!–this one was his wave, no question about it. He positioned himself right on the peak, wind-milled his arms, leapt to his feet, and without even thinking carved an effortless line down the face. He cranked out a bottom turn and then pulled up into a high line looking for a way in to something that did not yet exist. And suddenly there it was.

Behold the tube, the relentless, spinning, grinding core. The curl, like an immense quiff, arced out right over his head, and Ted found himself inside the "barrel," the elusive, elliptical waterfall formed by a breaking wave. Notwithstanding all the high-performance acrobatics of the younger generation, this was still surely the quintessence of surfing. If surfing had a soul it was right here, right now. Ted kept on driving down the line. With his right hand he scribbled a message over the face of the wave, instantly erased all over again as the wave kept on spinning, like the wheels of an immense one-arm bandit. The curtain came down over Ted. Maybe he went too high, because the next thing he knew he was tumbling around in the vortex, dragged up and flung down again. They call it the snake's eye, when the cylindrical core of a wave closes with someone inside. The eye blinked shut. On Ted. The evanescent architecture that is the interior of a wave–the "green room"–collapsed. Like a tall building being demolished by a wrecking ball. With Ted inside.

Which is when, Rabbit thought, he would have had the seizure and therefore drowned. Unconscious plus underwater equals death in fairly short order. Sometime later the body was recovered and he was cremated and then they paddled out for him on a serene day at Sunset and formed a circle and all held hands and said what an all-time surfer he had been and this is the way he would have wanted to go and then scattered his ashes out on the water where he would always be remembered.

This was pretty much how Rabbit Bartholomew, world champion pro surfer, had seen Ted's last wave, as he told me when I met him in Coolangatta, in Queensland. It was a scene that had replayed itself in his head, from time to time, over the last twenty years. He'd had it direct from Bernie Baker on the North Shore. Never questioned it. It was a good story. Made perfect sense. Ted would do just that, come what may.

Except that it didn't happen quite like that. In fact, nothing like that at all. Rabbit had been severely misinformed. Not that I blamed him. The North Shore, on the island of Oahu, Hawaii, was like a myth machine. Dreams and delusions proliferated like waves. Not too many of the inhabitants cared about the more complicated truth. Everybody lied, to themselves and others. And they had good reason, in certain circumstances, to avert the gaze. The code of omertà. The North Shore could legitimately lay claim to some of the greatest breaks on the planet. But it was for sure a place of heartbreak too.

2.

Ted was the epitome of a never-say-die guy. Then, in 1997, he died. I wrote his obituary for a London newspaper. Edward George William Omar Deerhurst, Viscount–and would-be world champion surfer. I wrote about his life and his death, but I didn't mention the times we went surfing together, or how he gave me one of his boards, or the Christmas party at Pit Bull's house, or that unforgettable night he took me to the Femme Nu nightclub in Honolulu.

I used to write about surfing for a living. Born in London, I had a recurrent dream as a kid of an apocalyptic tsunami sweeping up the Thames, wreaking havoc, drowning friends, family and teachers, while I alone surfed to salvation aboard a passing tree trunk or door. The bastard love child of the Beatles and the Beach Boys, I parlayed my dreams of conquering giant waves into a job as surfing correspondent to *The Times* of London, then *The Independent*—which took me to Hawaii and beyond, following the pro circuit around the world, and therefore bumping into Ted many times on far-flung shores. But eventually I stopped writing about surfing. I was all written out where waves were concerned. In my less footloose, turquoise-tinted job as lecturer at Cambridge University, I wrote about Napoleon or Brigitte Bardot or Lee Child instead. But I always thought I could still write something about Ted. Because even though he was a surfer, at the same time he wasn't just a surfer. He wasn't a loser, he was never that, he was more not-quite-yet-a-winner. He was a modern Don Quixote, he was a heroic failure, he was a miracle of persistence, a visionary, an idealist, a dreamer. The top surfers (take Kelly Slater, for example, eleven times world champion) were really nothing but surfers. They were 100% surfer. Pure and unalloyed. They had to be. Ted, on the other hand, was barely a surfer, he was only ever clinging on by his fingertips to that mad, mysterious and mystic status. He always seemed to have something else going on in his head at the time, beyond the simple yet impossible ambition to become the number one surfer on the planet—the dream of a chivalric golden age perhaps, or a mad quest, or a better world, or the perfect woman, or all of the above simultaneously. I almost forgot to say, he was a fundamentalist where romance was concerned. He really believed that love would save him. And that it would make him a better surfer too.

Then, too, there was something about the numerous, conflicting accounts of his death that never ceased to mystify me. It was not so much that there was a piece of the puzzle missing, more that there were too many puzzles with pieces scattered around the world.

Someone, I thought, ought to write something about Ted. To get to the bottom of the mystery. Maybe me. But I only knew him for the last decade of his abbreviated life. And when I thought about the vast network of people he knew and whose lives he had touched or who had touched him, I was acutely aware of the immensity of the task. I once read that if you really wanted to "beam up" someone, all those trillion or so cells and the unlimited stack of memories, you would need information enough to fill hard disks from here to the moon and back. Trying to reassemble the disparate parts of Ted's life—to stick together all the clues to his death—felt a bit like that. If I wanted to know anything, I had to know everything. If I wanted to work out what happened to him at the end I had to go right back to the beginning. His whole life was a clue. So I did nothing but think about it and prevaricate, for a decade or two, off and on.

After I wrote his obituary I heard from Ted's mother, Mimi, in Santa Cruz. Because this was back in the nineties, she didn't read it online. It took months for the story to reach her. And then more time for her to put pen to paper and write back to me. But she told me how moved she had been to read about her son's career, his adventures and mishaps, and asked could I possibly drop in on her the next time I was in California, where she was then married to a man called Blankenhorn, and living on North Pacific Avenue. Several months later I was in California so I called her number and I spoke to Mr Blankenhorn, who told me that Mimi had "passed" not long before. Later, I heard that Ted's father, the Earl of Coventry, had died too. He had no siblings, so that was about it for Ted's family I thought. It felt like the end of the road where the Ted story was concerned.

Then Duncan Coventry got in touch. His father had once said to him that "if seven people drop dead and another four don't have sons," then he would be the next Earl. He was around 757th in line for the throne. But, more importantly, cousin to Ted. He had never met Ted but he was inspired by his example and he wanted to know if I might consider writing Ted's life story. I went to meet him at a pub in Bristol to talk it over. It was early 2017. We were approaching the 20th anniversary of Ted's death. He reminded me a lot of Ted, only younger, taller and (obviously) alive. He had a son called Ted (or "Young Ted"). When he went surfing he felt as if he had Ted perched on his shoulder like a parrot, offering advice and steering him through stormy seas. He was the man behind a Facebook page in the name of Ted too.

Finally I went and stayed at his house in Devon, in the southwest corner of England, to examine some of the Deerhurst archives. It didn't surprise me that a popular rebellion had started right here, at the village church, back in 1549. The parishioners decided they wanted their old Latin prayer book back. They didn't like the new one, in English (which may have been too Protestant for their taste). Naturally they went and laid siege to Exeter. I had a feeling that Ted would have approved. He was a rebel and a malcontent too.

The rebellion was ruthlessly put down. Mercenaries were sent in and the rebels were all slaughtered. It's what happens to rebels.

3.

LOCATION: a Victorian terraced house in Newnham, Cambridge, UK

TIME: approx 3 a.m., one morning in May 1994

The phone rings. A groggy hand reaches out, picks up the receiver.

OPERATOR: Will you accept a transfer charge call from Hawaii?

ME: What? Who?

TED (breaking in): It's me, Ted!

OPERATOR: Will you accept the charge, sir?

ME (assuming it's some kind of emergency): Oh, OK, yeah, put him on.

OPERATOR: Go ahead, caller, you're connected.

TED: Andy, you're going to be kicking yourself in a minute.

ME: I'm already kicking myself. What's up?

TED: You remember how I told you I was going to find the perfect woman?

ME: What? You're calling about that? Ted, it's 3 a.m. here!

TED: And you remember how you didn't believe me? You were being your usual skeptical self, do you remember that?

ME: Look, Ted, right now, I can't remember what day it is.

TED: Well, now you are going to have to eat humble pie, my friend. Because I have actually found her.

ME: Who?

TED: The perfect woman. Her name is Lola.

ME: Come on. No one is called Lola. You made that up.

TED: Ye of little faith. Seeing is believing, so you'd better get your ass over here and see her for yourself.

ME: Funnily enough, I was sort of thinking about coming back in a couple of months. You know, after term finishes.

TED: A couple of months!? Can't you get here faster than that? I can't wait for you to meet her. You are going to love her. She works in a nightclub in Honolulu.

ME: A nightclub. What kind of a nightclub?

TED: Just get here and see for yourself, will you? And stop with all the Grand Inquisitor stuff!

ME: Yeah, I can just imagine how the Spanish Inquisition used to get phone calls in the middle of the night from the guys they were interrogating. I bet they didn't accept reverse charges though.

TED: Don't be bitter, man. Remember what I told you about my exacting specifications where the perfect woman is concerned?

ME: Ridiculous. I told you, it's anatomically impossible.

TED: Lola fulfils all the requirements. And more.

ME: In your dreams.

TED: Seriously.

ME: OK, OK, you win, I'd better come and see for myself.

TED: I knew you would want to see Lola.

ME: If I promise to come, will you stop calling me in the middle of the night?

TED: I'm in love. And you know what?

ME: What?

TED: She loves me. She told me so. Andy, this is the real thing. At last.

This was the first time I heard the name of Lola. Something told me it wouldn't be the last.

4.

I always thought New York would be the death of Ted.

But probably not on the mean streets of 1980s Manhattan. I remember that you didn't venture out in Central Park at night unless you actually wanted to get raped and murdered and sliced up. If you took the subway, close friends would ask if your room was available for rent. Natives taught me how to walk down the street in such a way that the bad guys would pick on some other poor devil, naively ill-prepared. It was that period, the era of *Death Wish* and *Taxi Driver*, when Sam Fussell, landing in the city for the first time, spoke (in *Muscle*) of wanting to reconstruct his own body in the form of robust armour plating, à la Schwarzenegger. This was the ultimate urban jungle. There was a ruthless, Darwinian quality to so much cement. You had to be just as hard. It was the exact opposite to being dumped in the middle of some far-flung wilderness and being expected to survive on your own, surrounded by pitiless, sabre-toothed predators: but otherwise it was similar.

But having a surfboard tucked under one arm in New York was almost like a magic wand or a cloak of invulnerability. Or possibly a sign of madness. You were technically on the wrong coast, after all. Wasn't the surf some three thousand miles away, due west? Muggers and murderers kept away from you. You were safe. Touched by grace or greatness. At least on land. It was the closest thing to walking on water and passers-by eyed you with something approaching reverence, awe or fear. There were occasional acts of kindness, the giving of alms, an exchange of glances, a secret camaraderie. We were like wandering medieval mystics, kin to the Buddha himself, throwing ourselves on the unpredictable mercy of fate.

Our paths might have crossed then. I was staying somewhere on 32nd Street, an indeterminate nowheresville that wasn't even a neighbourhood, or barely, sharing a shabby apartment with a Swiss purveyor of artworks and a ginger cat. I remember trying to hail a cab, aiming for Nicaragua, standing on the sidewalk with my surf bag slung over one shoulder. In vain. In the end a guy in a pick-up stopped for me. Ted was sleeping on a couch in the room of an NYU student, in one of those blocks near Washington Square. Further down Bleecker Street towards 6th Avenue Bob Dylan performed in the Fat Black Pussy Cat (or he had) and John Coltrane played (or had) in the Blue Note. And Ted was scraping a living working as a waiter at the Hard Rock Café. While dreaming of the day he would rule the world (at least that part of it that consisted of sand, sea and people in shorts).

There are sensible places to go surfing around New York. I've been to one or two of them. You hop on the train from Penn Station that takes you out to Long Island. You don't have to go all the way to East Hampton, or further still, to Montauk, appealing though those waves may be. Long Beach will do. Lots of very fine waves there too. I've seen it at six to eight feet and cranking. A great thundering beast of a wave on the right day. Far Rockaway, so I have heard from locals, is also acceptable. Take the subway. The Jersey shore, I'm told, is a regular treasure trove of good waves, on the right day.

But none of the above was good enough for Ted. "Long Island!" he would say. "Who needs Long Island? Is that even in New York?" Well, of course it was, politically, geographically, in any way that made sense. But Ted had to live the myth. He embraced the contradiction: "To come here and see the New York skyline while riding Australian-sized waves" (as he said in an interview). He basically wanted to surf down 5th Avenue. He wanted to surf the Empire State Building. He wanted to pull a bottom turn around the corner of Wall Street. And the closest he was going to get to owning the whole of New York and feeling it throb beneath his fins was to surf in the harbour. He would step out of a morning and troop over to Christopher Street and hop on the 1 train down to the Financial District. There he would board the Staten Island ferry. Others would be buttoned-up, smart, besuited, neatly pressed and creased, their shoes freshly polished and gleaming. They didn't wear hats any more, this wasn't *Mad Men*. Or, in a way, maybe it was.

Ted was already wearing all the right kit, by the way, either shorts and t-shirt (or rash vest) or, in a cooler season, a full-on 5mm wetsuit with gloves and hoodie. A wetsuit on the subway. And he was barefooted. Maybe he could have afforded shoes but he chose not to wear them. Obviously no one was going to mess with this guy–a holy fool perhaps? Was this obscure craft not also a weapon of some kind? Bigger after all than any mere blade or gun, more of a lance if anything. Clearly he was going to do battle, like a knight of old. But with what or whom?

Ted was 5' 9" with a slim build, but he would always stand out in a crowd. The long blonde curls probably helped. A little bit Errol Flynn, a little bit Ryan Gosling, with a dash of hippy for good measure. "This is my path," he wrote around this time, "it feels right."

So anyway he is on the ferry and the ferry is crossing the busy waterway between Manhattan and Staten Island. Remember, New York is nothing but a bundle of islands, loosely strung together with bridges and tunnels. When you look it squarely in the eye, it's mostly water. Like Venice. Like the planet. Like human beings, come to think of it. So, as I say, he is on the ferry, leaning against the rail, with New Jersey to starboard, and Brooklyn and Governors Island to port, and there coming up ahead is the Statue of Liberty, but then, suddenly, he is not on the ferry any more. To the astonishment of fellow passengers, with some kind of whooping war cry or sheer scream of unalloyed rapture, he goes flying off, leaping far out into the water, taking care to throw his surfboard out there ahead of him. Then he would reacquire the board and start paddling, with a quick wave of reassurance over his shoulder–"It's OK, I'm not committing suicide!"–in search of his wave.

I never saw it, but he stoutly maintained that, on the right day at the right time, a small but perfect wave would rise up, unbidden, from the depths, or rather the shallows, around the small island on which the Statue of Liberty stands. From here you look back towards Manhattan. Riding this rare and mysterious peak thrusting up towards heaven, known only to the cognoscenti, an elite of true fanatics, it must have seemed, with the skyscrapers of the great city in your sights, and the blue sky above, in the shadow of Liberty herself, and screeching seagulls swooping around you, as you weaved in and out of passing ships, and under the gaze of bewildered tourists, that you had taken possession, no matter how briefly, and therefore for all time, of the whole of New York. If Manhattan was a ship, figureheaded in those days by the Twin Towers, then Ted was something like a pirate, walking his own plank. If it was a whale then Ted was a harpoonist.

But now that I stop to think about it, maybe it wasn't so much that he wanted (as he once said) to "own" New York. It was rather that he was disowning it–this, the most massive little chunk of real estate on the planet, as if he was saying, a board and your shorts, that's all you really need. All those soaring pillared and porticoed temples of acquisitiveness, the whole of this mighty metropolis, he would give it all up–like the title he inherited–for just one moment of immortality.

Maybe Ted should have been concerned about those passing ships or sharks or pollution. He wasn't. He was blissfully unconcerned. He felt he really was immortal. For as long as the wave lasted.

5.

I finally met Ted in the summer of 1989. I was on honeymoon and he was on the opposite of a honeymoon. He was divorced from Susan, then partnered up with Debbie, then unpartnered all over again, and lonesome. "I need a babe," he said. He was explicit about it. He was explicit about everything. "I think it'll help my surfing."

He was always honest about his feelings (sometimes too honest, for my money). Whereas I was already living a lie. Although we had only got married a week or so before, my "photographer" and I were keeping it under our hats. We wanted to look like pros, not lightheaded newlyweds. I was writing the words, she was taking the pictures. It was strictly business. She had a massive Canon camera with telephoto lens to prove it too. Which we had somehow wangled out of Canon, in London, before setting off, for free. We were supposed to be writing a story about our surfari around all the west coasts of Europe, or as many as we could hit, for *The Sunday Times*.

Heading south from Brittany towards Spain, guided by a map designating the best waves, we arrived in Lacanau, west of Bordeaux, to discover that the place had been taken over by Quiksilver. They had colonised the entire beach with marquees and stages and pennants and music, giving it the feel of some medieval jousting tournament. Were the t-shirts not like a shield, emblazoned with obscure heraldry? Were waves not "white horses"? All it needed was Ivanhoe and Robin of Locksley and Maid Marion. I was lost and a guy with a radiant helmet of long, wavy blond hair directed me to the press tent. They gave us a luxurious room at a golf club hotel and five-star treatment. All expenses paid. All I had to do was write an article about the event. Deal, I said. With my photographer taking the pictures. For that week we would awake to the sound of birds tweeting and the sight of endless free croissants au beurre and café au lait.

I bumped into the guy with the wavy blond hair again at a beachside cafe looking out over the break. It was a small town, you were always bumping into people. So I thanked him. He introduced himself. He was in the contest and he explained how he used to be an amateur, representing the UK, but now was trying to make it on the pro circuit, run by the ASP (the Association of Surfing Professionals). He needed to climb up the rankings, to accumulate points, to win the surfing equivalent of a Grand Slam, to make an impact. It had been a bit of a struggle thus far, apparently, over a number of years, but he was hopeful that this summer would be the breakthrough for him. He struck a brave, optimistic note. That was when he told me about his "babe" theory. One guy, one board, one wave, that's all you need, some said. The "one guy" on his own part of it made no sense to Ted. A guy and a gal made way more sense. Ted and "a hot chick giving me non-stop sex for the whole Pro tour."

It sounded simple enough, but I felt bound to point out to him that according to Freud's potentially frustrating theory of "sublimation" he had it all wrong.

"Really?" he said.

"According to Freud anyway," I said.

"Just remind me how that works, 'sublimation,'" he said.

"Freud would say, don't have sex before the big match."

Ted looked at me askance. "Come on!" He had not encountered this seemingly puritanical approach before. He was pure hedonist. Nothing else made much sense to him.

"Seriously."

"Why on earth would he say that?"

"His idea was that all this massive sexual energy that you have, under the general heading of 'desire,' can be re-channelled into other endeavours. Repurposed. I think it's in *Civilisation and its Discontents*. Where do you get civilisation from? Answer: repressing all this desire and shoving it more in the direction of building bridges or tall buildings. Science or art, whatever. I think the word 'cathexis' is in there too."

"Cathexis?"

"Yeah, I'm never sure what that means though. But look, take surfing for example. Sublimation theory would say, I think, that if you want to be a great surfer you have to be a bit a monk and deprive yourself of congenial female company, go solo, and then all of that pent-up libido of yours will go straight into riding the waves instead. Then you'll become the great surfer you always wanted to be. But it requires sacrifices."

Ted look straight at me, taking it all in. "No sex?"

"You've got it."

He paused and reflected. "No," he said, decisively, with a shake of his head, blond locks flying. "I've tried that. It doesn't work. I'm already living like a monk." Freud was dismissed. Frustrated, Ted bombed; all he needed to do was score. It was logical, almost tautological. "Anyway if Freud is right then you're sunk. You've got someone. I can see it in your face."

Ted had a point. He always had a point. He was a good arguer and stuck to his guns and would have made a good lawyer. He would listen politely for a while and then say the opposite. I'm not sure I ever managed to persuade him of anything. I was having a great honeymoon in the golf hotel, with everything you could eat and drink to boot, but my surfing was not perhaps everything it should have been. Ted was advanced, nigh on virtuoso level; I was more intermediate wannabe. I remember one low point when the women's contest was going on and I decided to go out further down the beach. The surf was pumping and after a couple of spectacular wipe-outs and getting caught in the rip I somehow ended up bang in the middle of the women's contest. "Would the surfer in the blue wetsuit please get out of the water!" boomed the voice over the PA. At very high volume. I was that surfer in blue. I paddled way off and slunk out of the water and tried to cover my tracks. "Ha! Who was that kook?" I said, loudly, to anyone who would listen, having changed back into civilian kit. But Ted's words lingered in my mind. I was cursed by extreme happiness. I was too blissed out for my own good. I was suffering from satisfaction.

I ran into him next in Hossegor, further to the south, the second leg in what was becoming known as the French "Triple Crown," a would-be European rival to the Hawaiian Triple Crown. We were having dinner in the Dôme, a fairly classy non-beachside restaurant–my photographer (i.e. clandestine bride), Claudette and I. Claudette was a bright young PR woman who was liaison for Quiksilver or Billabong or one of those brands. Very helpful, very cheerful. She tended to wear shorts and a tight t-shirt, her brand name emblazoned on her chest. We were having a high old time, the three of us. I had a notion of sharing the secret of our marriage and everything, but she was a PR woman after all, probably not a great idea. My wife excused herself to go to the bathroom.

"Do we need her?" Claudette said bluntly when she had gone.

"How do you mean?" I said. We were speaking French at the time and maybe I was misunderstanding her drift.

"I mean, can't you get rid of her? You know, so we can be more together, *toi et moi*? Tu me plais, tu sais." She had her hand on my thigh under the table and was stroking it enthusiastically.

I kind of dabbed my forehead with a napkin and looked desperately into the beyond. She was attractive and fun, no question, Claudette, but come on! I'd only just got married. And not even announced yet. In terms of instantaneous betrayal, it'd be about on a par with Prince Charles and Diana. A phrase uttered by one of the lads at the wedding sprang to my mind. "Why does anyone get married? Because otherwise you'd miss out on adultery!" Yeah, funny, man. However, I thought it struck the wrong note right then and it still did. On the other hand, I didn't want to give offence. Claudette being so nice and all. Dilemma. The photographer was returning to the table. Just then I spotted my saviour at a nearby table. "Hey, Ted!" I yelled, with relief. "Get over here!"

He was on his own. So he wandered over. "Let me introduce you," I said. "Claudette, meet Ted." Ted smiled. At least I wouldn't have to get divorced even before I was known to be married. It was a bond between us. We were like a small mutual help society.

Inevitably, I saw Ted in Biarritz too, the next stop on the tour, deep in Basque country, down near the Spanish border. You couldn't exactly miss him. He had a classic surfer look, but at the same time no other surfers looked exactly like him. With the flying long locks he looked like a kind of icon perched on the bonnet of a Rolls Royce or the figurehead of a ship maybe. I was driving a Volkswagen Golf, I remember.

It was just after one of the heats. There was this little spot a kilometre out of town, a bay, where the wave was perfectly formed and was cranking out assembly line models one after another. I was doing my job, keeping an eye especially on any British surfers. Good material for the article. Ted agreed it was his kind of wave, but he didn't make it through. I thought he deserved a better result and was hard done by. Maybe even discriminated against. The French Triple Crown was tailor-made for Ted, but he had bombed out.

"I'll be ok when I get to Hawaii," he said, pulling off his competition vest. "I'm better in big surf." He had an idea that the huge and hairy Hawaiian waves would finally sort out the men from the boys.

"How did it work out with Claudette?" I asked. It was blatant curiosity, of course. But there was more to it than that. I really wanted to know whether Freud had it all wrong.

"I got hosed," he said. It was a phrase he used a lot. Not one I was familiar with. But I worked out that "getting hosed" was the opposite of ideal.

"What happened?"

"We really hit it off. OK, so maybe she was drinking a little too much. But I wasn't making her or anything. She was the one ordering. I drove her home. We stopped on the beach in the moonlight. God, it was so romantic. We were kissing and cuddling. Man, she was all over me."

I was impressed, in a way, by how quickly Claudette had switched her affection from me to Ted. Some sort of undirected spontaneous overflow of feeling. Why didn't this sort of thing happen to me *before* I got married?

"You lucky bastard," I said.

He grinned, but the smile was inflected with melancholy. "We stopped for another drink somewhere. And then we drove back to her place."

"Problem solved." He was drying his hair at the time. Which took a while. It consisted of him bending over with his head down and shaking his hair around in the breeze like a particularly shaggy dog. Leaving me hanging. "Wasn't it?"

"Oh," he said, "she passed out. Flopped down on the bed and went into a coma. I gave her a gentle nudge but she was too far gone."

"What did you do?"

"I made sure she was still breathing, propped her head up on the pillow, tucked her in, and vamoosed. Spent the night in the car. Listening to the sound of the surf."

"Jesus."

"You know what kept going through my head afterwards?"

"No."

"We could have made love on the beach. Under the stars. It was a perfect night for it. I blew it. Driving back to her place—what was I thinking? You know what, you're always learning."

At the level of theory, Ted scored high. Ted vs Freud and Freud placed nowhere. But only because, at the level of actual surfing, Ted's graph in Biarritz was still not going up and to the right. No girlfriend and no decent results either. He had had maximum sublimation, with extra torment thrown in for good measure, and still the winning formula eluded him. But there was one other British surfer who was competing in the French Triple Crown. His name was Martin Potter, aka "Pottz." Given that waves are so inclined to dump you and then stomp on you for good measure (a regular occurrence known as the *wipeout*), Pottz had developed a system for skimming over the surface. He flew over the waves. Hovered. I even wrote an article about the "aerial" moves he was pulling off (and the so-called "floaters" where he appeared to perch uncannily on the crest of the wave as if suspended by invisible wires). He was semi-invincible. Pottz won at Biarritz, scooped the Triple Crown, and was in pole position to take the title this year. A Brit, born in Northumberland (even if he had surfed mainly in South Africa and Australia and, unlike Ted, had never competed in the British amateur team), who might yet become world professional surfing champion. Maybe he was sublimating more than the average, but I doubted it. He was just more sublime. Pottz was my passport to the giant waves of Hawaii. He was all over the surfing magazines already, adorning the front cover of *Surfer.*

But I was really rooting for the underdog, the longshot, the loner, the unsung hero. Ted. Pottz had earned around a million dollars in prizes and endorsements. I'm not sure he even knew Ted existed. Ted, the eternal amateur, was going back to his job as a waiter to try and earn enough to get to Hawaii.

6.

"Ted? You mean *Lord* Ted! The 'Lord on a board'."

This, from some fellow reporter, when we were discussing the great mystery of Ted's results, or the lack of them. It took me a while to realise that Ted was Viscount Edward George William Omar Deerhurst, only son and heir of the Earl of Coventry. Ted himself forgot to mention it. He certainly wasn't bragging about it. If anything he was trying to forget. Like someone who joins the Foreign Legion to get over a break up, he wanted to put the romance of his own ancestry out of his head. Surfing was a way of erasing history, about as far as you could get from (landlocked) Coventry, but the past kept on coming back to haunt him.

The West Coast was in his blood, on his mother's side.

Mimi Medart would have been six years old and living in St Louis when the first wave of Japanese warplanes flew over Turtle Bay, on the northern tip of the island of Oahu, in December 1941, bearing down on Pearl Harbour, and about to sink a significant portion of the American navy, thereby propelling the United States into the Second World War, just as Winston Churchill had been urging. She was too young to worry about it and war still seemed a million miles from St Louis. And her father, William Sherman Medart, was too concerned with making hot dogs to worry too much either. He started small but he grew big. He made the best hot dogs, everybody said so. Not to mention hamburgers—the kind that Wimpy (Popeye's friend) and Homer Simpson loved to gulp down in a single swallow. There were a lot of potential hot dog consumers in the United States, an appetite undiminished (perhaps even increased) by war. William Sherman Medart became a "hotdog millionaire" (and the American waistline kept on expanding). For good or ill, he was a pioneer of the fast-food revolution.

By the age of fifteen Mimi had decided to become a ballerina. That was about as far away as she could get from hot dogs: the discipline and austerity of the leotard, the barre, the pirouette, and the fouetté. She used to love a good hot dog too, like anyone else, but after a childhood in which hot dogs were perpetually on offer for breakfast, lunch and dinner, her enthusiasm for them had begun to wane. She wanted to put some space between her and the realm of the hot dog. Ballet seemed to her like the answer to her prayers. She was tall and slim and graceful.

The Medarts had acquired a house on a hill in Palo Alto overlooking the Pacific. Little Mimi (as she soon became known, having been christened Marie Farquhar-Medart) went to sleep to the sound of waves gently unfurling on the shore, a soft susurration guaranteed to serenade her off to dreamland. She loved the changing colors and the moods of the sea, its never-ending parade of waves that put her in mind of dancers at the Moulin Rouge in Paris (she had never been there but she thought she knew what it must be like). She aspired to that kind of fluidity—to be like a fish in the sea, flashing silver in the sun, or a bird in the air soaring and swooping. Pure motion and energy, with no resemblance whatsoever to a cylindrical meat product. This is what she found in dancing. She trained hard and was soon recruited to the Los Angeles corps de ballet.

It was when they were performing in Deauville in 1951 and she was a bare sixteen years old that she caught the eye of the young King Farouk of Egypt, in fez and military uniform, who had briefly torn himself away from the pleasures of the casino (he once said that "Soon there will be only five reigning monarchs left in the world: the kings of England, hearts, clubs, spades and diamonds"). She was disporting herself on the beach and clad only in a bikini at the time, displaying a sylph-like figure to impressive effect. She said, "Delighted to meet you, your majesty," and retreated, receding like a tide. He deluged her hotel room with gladioli but was soon to become ex-King Farouk and would eventually die of over-eating in exile in an Italian restaurant. It would not be long before the ballerina met her prince.

George William Coventry was universally known as Bill (even Ted called him Bill rather than, for example, "Dad"). He was born in a house that was the size of a castle. Croome Court, in the county of Worcestershire, was an elegant country pile in the Palladian style, built out of creamy stone and set in an estate landscaped by Capability Brown, equipped with its own "temple."

The Coventry family went back centuries, to an era of barons and knights, to Lancelot and Guinevere (at least, in Ted's mind). The original Coventry had something to do

Croome Court (by Richard Wilson, 1758)

with Dick Whittington and his cat. The archives testify to a "William Coventrie of ye Citty of Coventrie" from around the time of Chaucer, and a Henry de Coventre before him. Subsequent Coventrys were woven into recorded history, inspiring a poem by Andrew Marvell and admiring remarks in an August 1657 entry of the diary of Samuel Pepys ("Sir William Coventry is the man and nothing done till he comes"). They lived through Plantagenets and Tudors, the Spanish Armada, rebellion, uprisings, wars (Civil and uncivil) and the Industrial Revolution, and dutifully attended Balliol College or Christ Church, Oxford. Perched upon the manifold branches of the family tree were warriors and Cardinals, lawyers and ambassadors, members of the Privy Council and Lord Keepers of the Great Seal—all loyal servants of the Crown. Portraits of them hung in baronial halls. Scandals, banquets, mistresses, top hats abounded. Streets and workhouses were named after them. Of course, there were occasional cads and wastrels, almost certainly scoundrels. On the other hand there was at least one Master of the Bath House. Perhaps one of them was the real William Shakespeare. And Coventry was Camelot ("Anything's possible!" Ted would say). In any case, the Coventrys were fruitful and multiplied. The original parish church of Croome had the figure of a knight painted on one of its northern windows, dressed as a Crusader, in a coat of mail and a white mantle emblazoned with a red cross, and bearing a shield Argent. Family motto, "Candide et constanter" (candidly and constantly).

Bill's father (also George William) died, "killed in action," at Dunkirk in 1940. According to his diary, he was in his element. "We are fighting at last & I must say I enjoy

Candidly and constantly

most of it immensely......all so exciting." But the 10th Earl especially appreciated the camaraderie: "men whom you know will stand by each other whatever happens. I don't mean you think will; you know because we've been through enough to have tested it. It makes you rather proud of being considered worthwhile as there is no pretence out here." He was blissfully unconcerned for his own safety. "C'est la guerre!" he wrote in the midst of battle. Here is his entry for May 19: "I'm keeping v. fit & really enjoying myself a lot although it's harder than anything I thought possible."

Another observation: "it's rather like when your hounds have hunted extra well & you feel thoroughly happy with life." Ted's grandfather was one of the thousands of British troops retreating in the face of the advancing German tide, many of whom were rescued by the heroic flotilla of little boats that came across the Channel to pick up the army and carry them back to England to fight another day. But Bill senior, then thirty-nine, a lieutenant serving in the Worcestershire regiment, didn't feel like retreating. He was having too good a time. So he stayed behind to fight the entire Germany army on his own. And the Luftwaffe. On May 27, 1940, somewhere in the vicinity of Givenchy, he was shot to pieces then annihilated by a shell, leaving nothing but a poignant memory and a title. Bill junior was just six years old. At the exact time his father was killed, Bill, previously Viscount Deerhurst (as was the tradition, a "subsidiary" title to the earldom created in 1697, named after a village in Gloucestershire), became the 11th Earl of Coventry, with a seat in the House of Lords. His mother, the Countess of Coventry, promptly found herself a replacement husband and Bill was duly packed off to Eton. Where he would have to sink or swim, on his own.

There were occasional visits home, but from the age of six he had to make his own way in the world. Growing up in the middle of the Second World War, with a dead hero for a father, he saw life in essentially martial terms, where you were either victorious or vanquished, friend or foe, and everything was either defense or attack, a matter of strategy and struggle and amassing superior forces. He took up the rapier and the épée at school and won a bronze medal in the Public Schools Fencing Championships of 1951. After Eton he went to Sandhurst, the army academy for officer training. World War III couldn't be that far away and he wanted to be ready. He was commissioned in the Grenadier Guards. Then he met Mimi. She was performing in London and he went backstage to meet her. The ballerina and the Grenadier Guard.

In 1955, at the age of twenty, Mimi was no longer just a ballerina: she was already (in the parlance of the era) a film "starlet." She had obtained a number of small roles in small films, and glossy stills were available through her publicist in Hollywood. At around the same time Bill was earning his bronze medal with a rapier, her father had fallen to his death, "in mysterious circumstances," from a hotel window in Paris, perhaps dispatched by either a jealous lover or a rival hotdog magnate, or both. In any case, by 1955, Mimi was in high demand. Senator-to-be Edward Kennedy was rumoured to be an admirer, as were senior members of the British Labour Party and even a representative of the Soviet trade delegation (i.e. a spy).

But Mimi fell for Bill. Maybe it was the Guards uniform. Or the rapier. She was touché. After the obligatory whirlwind romance, they married in the same year, and Bill resigned his commission in the Guards. She didn't much fancy the great country estate, so they set up house in a flat in Mayfair, London. They were both just 21. They became staple fare of the gossip columns, and were photographed dancing the night away at clubs such as Brads and the Crazy E. Bill, not to be outdone, became a noted exponent of the Shake. They also drank a lot, especially Bill, champagne typically, or gin and tonic.

Maybe they slowed down a bit for the pregnancy. Ted was born in September of 1957. Which brought the Shake to a shuddering halt. Edward George William Omar, Viscount Deerhurst (the "George William" went back to the eighteenth century; the "Omar" came from no one knew where–Sharif? Khayyam?) was duly christened in the crypt of the House of Commons, followed by a reception in a gallery of the House of Lords, festooned with portraits of ancient Lords, one or two probably relatives. Ted might as well get used to it, they thought. It was his initiation. "He is the perfect baby," said Mimi, beaming. Lords and ladies cooed. Little Ted, aged seven months, had a quiff and his proud mother was wearing an immense and elegant hat. The Soviet ambassador of the period, a Mr Jacob Malik, tickled the lad under the chin and pronounced, "He looks typically British. I expect he will prefer whisky to champagne" and promised to send him a bottle of vodka, perhaps with a notion of recruiting him to the Reds.

Beyond the House of Lords, Bill, ex-Guardsman that he was, didn't adapt too well to peacetime. He was made for war. Perhaps, ex-eligible bachelor that he also was, he didn't adapt

Mimi and Bill in London, c. 1956

that well to fatherhood either. For one thing, he hadn't had a lot of practice. For another, his own father was not much of a role model, unless you wanted to go and get shot to pieces. He relied on being an old-style disciplinarian and sending his son off to boarding school as soon as humanly possible. The truth is that he didn't adapt that well to marriage either, tending to spend increasing amounts of time at the club, drinking with his gentleman friends where–as a staunch member of the Conservative Party–he would voice views and opinions about the great issues of the day, and then have a stab at a job in the City with a firm of stockbrokers. There were rumors of other starlets on his radar. Mimi and Bill were divorced in 1963. Irreconcilable differences.

Ted was just six at the time. According to the terms of the divorce settlement, the mother was awarded custody of the child, but on condition that he was brought up in England. It had to be England, not Scotland, or Wales, and especially not the United States. He was English, born and bred, and would remain so, said Bill. It was all about primogeniture, nothing to do with American mothers. But Mimi, having fallen out of love with the Earl of Coventry, was desperate to go and see her own family again, her mother in particular, who was now living in Santa Monica, Los Angeles. She went back to America for a couple of brief visits but always, abiding by the legally binding terms of the agreement, left young Edward behind, toiling away at his prep school, Woodcote House, in Surrey, where Ted earned the occasional caning from the headmaster for minor infractions of the rules. *Pour encourager les autres,* said the Beak, teaching Ted French and a greater sense of self-discipline at a stroke.

Mimi, a keen horsewoman herself, taught Ted to ride. There are charming early pictures of Ted and his horse. But when he was aged seven his horse threw him. Ted landed in a tangle on the ground. Then the horse proceeded to stomp on him too. No broken bones as such but a few hoof-shaped bruises. His mother didn't coo over him, she put him straight back in the saddle. Many years later in Hawaii he would say, "I guess I've been getting back on that horse ever since."

Bill, meanwhile, had been leading a torrid and turbulent life. Regularly thrown off his horse too. Almost the exact opposite of "Candider et Constanter," at least the constanter part. He had taken up with a nineteen-year-old drama student, Susan Templeton-Knight, but their engagement was broken off after nine months. On the professional front he had, in the course of just a few years, tried his hand at working as a porter for a Chelsea removals firm, a dress designer ("I have no training as a dress designer, but I know how I like women to look and I shall design instinctively"), a cosmetics salesman and president of a Panamanian-registered oil company, Middle East Oil Royalties ("I was very surprised at the offer of this job, but I can assure you I am expected to work jolly hard"). He had also been fined £50 after pleading guilty under the Prevention of Fraud act, dealing in shares and securities without a Board of Trade license, and had decided to abandon London and return to Worcestershire and Croome Court (or rather, by then, Earls Croome, nearby).

Perhaps his highpoint, professionally speaking, came when he tried out for the part of 007. He and Mimi had always moved in movie-making circles. They were on a par with film stars. And Bill certainly looked the part. So when Cubby

Mother and son

Broccoli was looking for a new James Bond to replace Sean Connery and he happened to bump into Bill at a party, he suggested he might like to audition. Bill was six foot three inches, [as elsewhere] with clean symmetrical features and a strong jaw. And he was adept with a sword. What else did you need? As it turned out, at least some aptitude for acting was required. Bill duly went along to the studios and auditioned bravely but he was hopeless at remembering his lines and went wooden in front of the cameras. Apart from that he might have made a better fist of 007 than George Lazenby or Roger Moore.

Then, in the summer of 1967, Mimi sought Bill out in Worcestershire where he had become an assistant personnel manager. She asked him, casually, didn't he think, now Ted was growing up (he was now nearly ten) that he would benefit by going for a "holiday" to California? Bill had no high opinion of the USA, but he couldn't see why he should not go for a month, before returning to start at Eton, Bill's old school, at the beginning of September. Mimi and Ted took ship for California. But they would not return in September, nor in October. Ted did not go to school at his father's alma mater in England. He started school in Los Angeles, in Santa Monica, at Lincoln Junior High, in the fall semester of 1967.

1.

Which explains why, half a century later, I went to see Tony Alva in Santa Monica, where he still lives. If I wanted to find out what happened to Ted in the end I needed to go right back to the beginning. To his schooldays. Tony and Ted were in the same year at Lincoln Junior High. It was not a school with a strict dress code: anything would do so long as you had a board (surf or skate) under one arm. "Ted never made it to SaMoHi [Santa Monica High]," Tony said in an email. "He got snatched away."

We met at Dog Coffee, which was formerly the Zephyr shaping shop. On the wall adjacent to the parking lot there is a giant mural of Jay Adams (who died in his thirties) skateboarding along the inside edge of an empty swimming pool at an improbable angle, observed by a bemused dog. "Ted loved this place," Alva said. "He knew it was special. It's why I brought you here." There were still classic surfboards adorning the walls, one highly polychromatic, with a dash of psychedelic, signed "Alva," together with skateboards. And a photograph of Alva, knees up around his chin, one hand gripping his deck, pulling off a fancy aerial manoeuvre on a green skateboard. A poster in the front window advertised a talk he had been giving there recently, under the heading "The Peaceful Warrior," in aid of www.1recovery.com.

I had once lived in Santa Monica too, in the 1980s, long after Ted had been legally whisked away. I was sharing a flat with an apprentice chiropractor, and had caught my first West Coast wave right there (I wasn't wearing a wetsuit, misled by so much hype and mythification, and the water in April was freezing, something the Beach Boys had neglected to mention—about on a level with Scotland). So I felt I was going back to my roots.

"Thank him for all the good times," my two sons had said to me. They had been glued to Alva's exploits in skateboard video games when they were growing up. He was and remains one of the most famous pro skaters in the world, one of the group of young trailblazers and technical innovators who become known as the "Z-boys" (after Zephyr) or "Dogtown boys" (after the neighbourhood). There is even a eulogistic documentary movie, by Stacey Peralta, *Dogtown and Z-Boys*, tracing their escapades around the streets and empty swimming pools of Venice Beach, and yet another feature film, *Lords of Dogtown*, giving it the full Hollywood treatment. They were the rock stars of urban surfing. Alva had long hair and a beard streaked with grey and dark glasses and while we sat in the cafe drinking black coffee (me) and organic lemonade (him) people would come up to him and ask him for his autograph or seek his advice in a tone of immense respect, almost awe. He was a man wholly devoid of arrogance who wanted to save young kids in trouble with drink or drugs or whatever. Get them on the right track. He had the scholarly air of a professor of skateboarding, if such a chimera should exist.

They met when Ted was only ten or eleven. Alva evoked a lost world in which kids ruled, entirely unsupervised by grown-ups. "I saw him out there eating it, slipping and sliding around," Alva said. Wandering the beach, Ted had seen surfers out on the break and had been entranced, bewitched. He'd never seen anything like it in England. To his eye it looked magical, miraculous, mythical. Like walking on water. Glowing–haloed–in the Californian sunshine, surely these were baggy-shorted gods among men? Naturally, he wanted to give it a try, but was trying to work it out on his own. He had heard surfers speak of "waxing" the board, so he had done just that, waxing it on the underside, as if it was a ski, to make it go faster in the water. But it's practically impossible to stay upright on a wet board with no wax on the deck. When Ted came out, looking crestfallen, after taking a beating and getting nowhere, Alva took pity and went up to him and said, "Dude, you might want to wax the other side the next time–it works a lot better." Ted had found a protector, a guru. Alva was the same age, but he looked older and was more experienced in the ways of the world and of the beach in particular.

Alva's mother was Dutch, but his father was Mexican, and he had dark hair and a rugged, sun-resistant complexion, in contrast with Ted's pale skin and fair hair. Alva senior was a boxer of some renown (a "Golden Gloves" champion) and he brought his son up to be capable of defending himself against all comers. "I was an alpha male," said Alva. "Ferociously competitive, it didn't matter what. I was small but I had a huge ego." He rose to become leader of the pack. He said it wasn't due to his ability, he just wanted it more than anyone else. Every now and then he would "bark" at Ted and Ted would be submissive and do as he was told. In return, if anyone ever gave the young Brit a hard time, Alva would step in and say, "Dude, if you want to get to him you have to go through me first." His aim, as he put it, was "to be actively calm and calmly active in trepidatious encounters."

Alva started out as a sidewalk surfer around eleven or twelve. He was the best in Santa Monica by the age of sixteen. By nineteen he was world champion and was already in the Guinness Book of Records. Like a gunslinger for hire, he would go from town to town looking for the best guy to beat. Ted tried his hand at skateboarding, but his first love was always surfing. He and Alva would stow their boards in the garage under Ted's house on 5th Street, just off Colorado, next to the old Sears building, only a few blocks up from the beach, where he lived with his mother and grandmother.

Now the terminus of the Santa Monica branch of the LA metro system stands where Ted once lived. Then, at the end of the 1960s and the beginning of the '70s Ted and Tony would pick up their boards (any dings carefully patched to keep the boards going), say goodbye to Ted's Ma (she would always give them both a hug and a kiss) and walk over the bridge to the pier in Pacific Ocean Park ("P.O.P" as they called it), eyeball the surf, and then paddle out together, laughing and splashing one another. Life, as Alva put it, "wasn't a bowl of cherries for sure," but out there on the ocean, beyond dry land, they created their own Shangri-La. For someone like Ted it was an escape from the conflict within his family and inside himself. He always had to put on a lot of zinc. Alva didn't. He had the bronzed, lined, weatherbeaten look that Ted could only dream of.

Ted's mother was "beautiful," Alva said. She radiated "kindness and calmness." And she approved of Ted's surfing.

His more authoritarian grandmother, in contrast, was tough on Ted. She was "sharp-tongued and quick to anger." She somehow blamed Ted for the misfortune of her daughter being a single mother living in a small house in Santa Monica on the verge of poverty rather than a globe-trotting ballerina, courted by kings. Everything was Ted's fault, she thought. He was like an anchor around her daughter's lithe and balletic legs. You could understand the thinking: her daughter sets off to England as the Countess of Coventry, and returns with a scruffy-haired beach urchin. It must have felt like something of a catastrophe, almost a tragedy. As if somebody or something had died.

Odd couple though they were, Tony and Ted became inseparable. Ironically, it was Ted who introduced Alva to the Zephyr store. Back then Santa Monica was divided into the more affluent North side, where they were from, and the poorer South side–"salt of the earth"–where the Zephyr store was. "Ted turned me on to the south side." Alva said he owed it all to Ted. "Without Ted I wouldn't have done it. He showed me the door." Alva was still protecting Ted even now he was dead. Maybe he still needed protecting. Alva was his guardian angel. Pity he hadn't been there in Hawaii too, when Ted really needed one.

Alva didn't know about Lola. But he knew a few of her precursors. One in particular. Ted's early love life in Santa Monica was–it could be said–tempestuous. Not a lot happened, but it was intense. At Lincoln Junior High Ted and Alva fell for three girls: Suzy Horne, Gloria Bartolucci and Heather Thomas. But mainly Heather Thomas. She was a body surfer and skateboarder and the movie-star girl of her year (the same year as Ted and Tony): blonde, blue-eyed, fair-skinned and increasingly shapely as the years went on. Alas she was, for that very reason, monopolised and guarded and ring-fenced by one of the jocks: Mike Hoper, a "gnarly guy," as Alva put it (even Heather Thomas described him as a "thug" with a resemblance to the young Marlon Brando who "would beat the shit out of you" if you looked at him sideways.)

Ted, aged fourteen, like some lovesick swain in a courtly love poem, admired and desired from afar. "She was beautiful," said Alva, "but untouchable." She was the first–other than his own mother–of the archetypal women who tent-poled Ted's life. Perfect, friendly even, but ultimately aloof and as unattainable as the moon. She already looked like an actress. Ted swooned but was forced to suffer the agonies of sublimation from an early age. Ted was a viscount, it was true, but in LA it was as if the feudal system was turned on its head: Heather Thomas was a grand and radiant Lady and he was only one of the peasants, with no chance of wooing let alone winning her.

Ted was not gay or bi, but he idolised males with just as much fervour as females. In Santa Monica Tony Alva was the grand seigneur to whom he bowed down and paid homage. A "lord of Dogtown." Edward George William Omar Deerhurst, future Earl of Coventry, was himself noble, but he saw others as the true nobility, an aristocracy of beauty or sheer mystifying god-given talent. In his mind he always saw himself–just as he had been in the Houses of Parliament at his own christening–surrounded by lords and ladies. Whereas he (to his way of thinking) was just one of the underlings. Feudalism never died, it just morphed and twisted and re-formed. Ted aspired to be a true lord and legend, and it was his fate to never quite make it, except as "Lord Ted" (which had more mythic appeal than "Viscount Ted"). Ted lived from 1957 to 1997 and he was living through not just four decades but a new Middle Ages. He professed to be egalitarian, but he had drifted into a realm that was as brutally competitive as they come, an arena that would become littered with the bodies of dead duellists.

"Nobody can tell you who your god is," Alva said.

Or goddess.

8.

Her place reminded me of the Alhambra in Granada–all light
and fountains and shade and terraces, setting off an elegant
castle or possibly several castles. She lived in Brentwood,
only a mile or two from Santa Monica. She was married to
a celebrity lawyer. Perhaps not all that surprising given that
Heather Thomas herself has been and still is a celebrity in her
own right. After Santa Monica High she studied at UCLA
School of Theater, Film and Television and went on to star
in such movies as *Zapped!* and *Cyclone*, but probably became
a legend thanks to her regular appearance in *The Fall Guy*,
the long-running television series of the 1980s, in which
she played Jody Banks, a fit, good-looking, blonde, kick-ass
adventurer. I saw a few episodes back in the day. So did Ted.
He was still in love with her.

I could understand that. I kept missing her because she
was away in Ohio getting her teeth fixed, which was a long
way to go to the dentist, especially considering there must
be a few around Hollywood. But he was doing a great job
and she had a terrific smile and looked, still, I could see, like
the embodiment of feminine perfection that Ted had always
seen her as. Despite getting hit by a car back in the '80s (Ted
was with her when it happened) and a cocaine habit she
picked up around the same time but overcame, she remains

the quintessential California Girl. She once appeared on the cover of a magazine under the heading "THE BEST BODIES IN HOLLYWOOD." But I should add, in fairness to her sheer diversity, that she is now also a screenwriter and a political activist, holding parties at her palatial home to support the Democratic party and oppose the current president and "everything that is ugly about America." She is not just a "Surfer Girl," as per the Beach Boys song, "I have watched you on the shore, Standing by the ocean's roar"–the girl who "made my heart come all undone." But she is that too.

By the age of fourteen, she was already working on television, interviewing celebrities in a program called "Talking with a Giant." At school she recalls a lunchtime menu of "reds" (downers), "blues" (uppers) and "whites" for studying. She was no idiot, that was for sure, and she studied (she was actually in an "accelerated class") and trained and worked out and did everything an aspiring actor ought to do. But the fact is that she was endowed with a massively advantageous genetic inheritance: she just looked the way a fourteen-year-old girl was supposed to look to the eye of the collective unconscious, which is to say in front of a television camera. And similarly to Ted's eye. She was quite simply *the* fourteen-year-old girl, but he could only admire and revere from a safe distance. She was surrounded not just by the feared older guy but by a cortege, a cordon sanitaire of minders and fans. There was no hope for him. She was in demand and she always would be.

And then one day he got to take her out for her birthday.

It was like a miracle. Grace descending from above. September 8, 1971. The gnarly boyfriend was ill and had let her down at the last moment. Her parents were fighting so much at the time they had forgotten all about her birthday. Ted stepped in and, in his modest, self-doubting way, volunteered to fill the gap and take her to the movies. He was shaken when she agreed. Sympathetic about the sick boyfriend and the negligent parents, but secretly thanking the gods who had smiled down upon him, Ted was finally living the dream.

It was probably the most intense evening of his young life. Heather, on the other hand, saw it as her due. This was normal. People were always taking her out to places and buying her nice things. Ted put on his best jeans and his favourite t-shirt. Afterwards they went for a pizza and a milkshake. "It was kinda embarrassing that my folks forgot," Heather said. "I wouldn't have shared that with anyone but Ted." At the end of the evening she thanked Ted (who, she noted, seemed to struggle to string his sentences together) and gave him a peck on the cheek and went back to her parents' house. Ted was on fire and couldn't sleep and the next day was telling Alva all about it. Even Alva was impressed.

"Ted was in love with me?" Heather said. "I had no idea!" Ted barely registered on her radar. He was "so sweet" and a "nice guy"–"a kid who liked to go down to the beach." But he was not a serious contender. "It was an innocent thing." They were just "good friends." She noticed–without ever understanding why–that "he was always sad." Much later he would come to visit her in hospital after her accident too, but she had a lot of visitors. "I'd open my eyes and it was a different boyfriend. Ted and I laughed about it." The first she knew of him being half-British was when he disappeared and people were trying to hide him from his pursuers. "He didn't seem

English—he blended in." But Ted never forgot her. The image of Heather Thomas was seared into his brain for all time.

Plato says that certain "forms" are fixed in our minds even before birth and everything else in our lives seems relatively imperfect by comparison, a flawed "copy" or pale "reflection" of the Real Thing, or Ideal. Going to the movie and having a pizza with Heather Thomas was like going straight up to heaven for Ted and then being flung back down again. When he called her up a few years later she agreed to become the poster girl for the Excalibur series of charity surf meets, held at different locations around the country. The winner of the contest would receive the sword, and Ted would continue to worship and adore (in vain) the unsurpassable princess and surfer girl of his imagination. Heather was one of the precursors of Lola, or Lola was an avatar of Heather.

Lincoln High, Heather Thomas said, was "ridiculously permissive." But possibly not in quite the way Ted had in mind.

She heard about his death from his mother.

She still kept a pair of Excalibur shorts to remember Ted by.

9.

It was in 1972 that they finally came for him. Mimi knew they were coming. Bill was on the warpath and he wanted his son back again. Ted, after all, was his only son and heir. He would, on the death of his father, become Earl of Coventry. He had to be brought up and nurtured in the land of his fore-fathers. The Coventry family had existed before America. And it must still come first.

According to Ted, his father was required by the terms of the trust he depended on to ensure that Ted was indeed brought up in England. No Ted, no money. Thus, one way and another, his country needed Ted. But did Ted need his country? And, when it came right down to it, was his country really Britain? In those few short years, he had become thoroughly Americanized. He loved Santa Monica, Venice Beach, the surfing, the bikes, the skateboards, the girls, the guys, the dash of Hollywood. "Ted never made a big deal out of his blue blood," Alva said. "He wanted to be one of the boys. He didn't want to be a rich dude. Or locked up in a school."

"I want to be an American," Ted wailed when he was apprehended. He didn't fancy grey skies and boarding school and cold showers.

In the summer of 1972, there were not just one but two private eyes on his trail. Like a pincer movement, and they were closing in. Closely followed by Bill himself. Somehow Ted got wind of it, maybe through his school. He confided in fellow surfer and skateboarder and Lincoln Junior High contemporary Gregory Evans, whose mother was English, so they were symmetrical. Up to this point they had only exchanged "Hey, dude" greetings. Now Ted poured out his heart and his fears. His fifteen-year-old friend could only comment, "It sucks that they want to take you away, man." Ted agreed that it sucked. So he dyed his blonde hair black and took a bus out of town. He was a fugitive from the law. He hid out in the hills, the nearby Big Bear mountains, where one of his friends' parents had a cabin. So they arrested his mother instead. "He really loved his mother," Alva said. "She was like a saint to him." Alva bravely intervened, a slight fourteen-year-old, meeting Ted's imposing father and trying to dissuade 007 from his planned course of action. He failed.

Ted followed developments from his mountain refuge through TV news bulletins. Which is how he came to see footage of his mother being led away in handcuffs and man-handled into a squad car. She had offended against the terms of the divorce settlement. From Bill's point of view, she had kidnapped his son. Technically, she was guilty of contempt of court. But Ted felt obscurely that, as his grandmother had always said, it really was his own fault. So he handed himself in. He took the bus back into town and presented himself at a police precinct.

"I'm the one you're looking for," he said.

He wasn't exactly arrested, but it must have felt like that. LAPD took him into so-called "protective custody."

Mimi was released, one out one in. There was a trial of sorts, a "hearing" before a judge. Ted was, in effect, convicted. Sentenced to prison i.e. England. Outside the courtroom, Ted announced to reporters and TV crews, "I wanna stay in America and surf with my friends."

Bill was waiting for him. "I don't want to go back to England," Ted said, calmly. "I want to be an American." Expecting, perhaps, that this statement of preference would be enough.

Bill, however, took no notice of what his son wanted or didn't want. The history of the Coventry family was bigger than both of them. It was Ted's destiny to carry on the line, not hang about on the beach with a bunch of West Coast ragamuffins and beachbums.

There is a picture of Ted being hauled back to England by his father. It appeared in the newspapers of the time. They're at the airport. Bill is towering over him and has a hand on his jacket, as if to stop him running off again. This is 007 after all. He is not going to let a mere kid off the hook. Ted looks aggrieved, anguished, indignant. As if he is being kidnapped all over again. By his own father. The thing that is not visible in the photograph, which is black and white, is the colour of Ted's hair. He had dyed it again, this time orange, in protest. It was the worst thing he could think of to do to his Dad at the time. Take that, Bill! Orange hair, how do you like it?

The return flight to London was frosty. Father and son did not speak to one another.

Back in England, embarrassed by how conspicuous he was, he tried to peroxide the orange out and restore his natural blond colour. By the time he started his first term at Millfield School in Somerset in September, he had green hair.

Son arrested by father and forcibly flown back to England.
With orange hair

"He took the spirit of Dogtown back to England," said Alva.

Susan, Ted's future wife, said, "He never grew after that. He just stopped growing." That is, he remained stuck at the height he was at age fifteen (5 foot 9 inches). But also, according to her, he sort of got stuck at that age, emotionally. Ted would be a fifteen-year-old boy for ever and ever. It's plausible. Naturally he would gravitate to a career in which he got to wear shorts all the time (and, to my knowledge, would only wear long pants for formal occasions). "The only difference," she said, "was that his hair curled. It was straight until then. Afterwards it was always wavy."

10.

I'd better mention the skiing, because it becomes relevant later on, when Ted decides to go snowboarding. Which, it turned out, was not such a great idea.

He learned to ski with Bill. He never called him "Father" or "Dad," just "Bill." Bill was OK with that. He took Ted skiing as part of his campaign to win Ted over to living in England. It wasn't as if you had to stay in England religiously. The French Alps, around Mont Blanc, were permitted.

Bill was an expert skier. He had learned when he was still at school, up in Scotland, which made everywhere else seem easy. And now he was passing on his skills to his one and only son. There is something beautiful and fundamental about that. Whether it's riding a bike or playing football or, as in this case, slaloming at top speed down mountains, it seems like it is the natural order of things for a father to pass on the baton of his experience to his son. They went to Flaine, in the Haute Savoie, suitable for skiers of different levels. It was vast, it was like you could ski across several countries. And Ted was a fast learner.

He couldn't wait to get off the nursery slopes and straight on to the "black" pistes favoured by his father. Ted was a natural. But Bill–the responsible father (who also didn't want to be slowed down too much)–wanted to make sure he didn't kill young Ted by letting him progress too fast, so he put him in the hands of a laid-back and very capable French ski instructor by the name of Serge Vaufrey. Bill shoved off and skied with his friends or relaxed in the bars and cafés on the slopes, while Ted was going to classes. But Ted didn't mind being dumped. Serge became his surrogate father. Ted was always looking for father figures to replace his actual father. Serge was knowledgeable, kindly and built like a bear, and, in effect, took over where Tony Alva left off. What Alva was to skateboarding and surfing, Serge was to skiing. He had a great tan, stubble, good teeth and years of accumulated wisdom. Ted would naturally fall in love with him. He would say later that he learned everything he knew about the mountains from Serge. It's just a pity that Serge didn't introduce him to snowboarding, but snowboarding at that point (the mid-70s) had barely taken off.

Ted and Bill went back to England. Time to go back to school. According to Bill. Ted got on the train and waved goodbye to his father. But as soon as Bill sauntered off, content that he had again done his duty by way of solo parenthood, Ted got off the train again and got on another train entirely. To Dover. Got on the ferry to France. Hitchhiked all the way back to Mont Blanc, through sleet and snow. Wet and cold. Took him several days. Sleeping in barns. Nobody knew where he was. His school trunks had arrived at school without Ted. Ted had run off again, just as he had run off in Santa Monica.

He hired a pair of skis and pointed his skis in the direction of Serge's log cabin in the woods.

"Serge, I want to stay with you." Young Ted panting and puffing at the door. Outside, a whiteout. A blizzard in the mist. "Can I?" Ted had made up his mind that Serge was a better father than his actual father. And high up in the Alps was better than England. Anywhere other than home.

"What a nice surprise, Ted," said Serge, in his highly accented English. "I thought you had gone back to England."

"I hate England," said Ted.

"Come and sit and let us talk."

Ted dried out and warmed up. Serge made him a mug of hot chocolate and they talked in front of the fire. Ted said how he loved the mountains and hated school, which felt more like prison, and he had decided to stay here and become a ski instructor just like Serge. If that was OK with Serge. Serge said that he thought it was a great idea and Ted would be perfect as a ski instructor: at some undefined point in the future. But, just for the time being, "What about your father?"

"He doesn't really love me," said Ted. "He just wants me to become an English lord. I don't want to go back to school, I want to stay here with you." He wept bitter tears.

Serge wrapped his huge bear-like arm around Ted's shoulders. "I will tell you something you don't know. Or don't realize. Or just don't want to know. I know your father. And I know that he really loves you and cares for you. Look at all the trouble he has gone to just for you. He goes to the West Coast of the United States. He flies you to England. He takes you here to the mountains. All of this he does because he loves you. He just does not know how to show his emotions, that is all."

Serge knew so much, perhaps he was right, Ted thought. He surrendered to the greater wisdom of the old man of the mountains. Serge called Bill back in England. Sighs of relief all round.

Serge and Ted strapped on their skis together and Ted went back to his prison in England.

11.

It's the hair that Mike Baker recalls even now, more than forty years on, from their first meeting. It took months before the colour faded. "Green hair would get you a degree of notoriety, even at Millfield," he said. Even if it was unintentional. "We all thought it was some new fashion from the West Coast, that maybe everyone out there had green hair, or other wacky colours. Something to do with the drugs maybe. Psychedelic. The hippy era, all things alternative. We really had no idea." The poet Charles Baudelaire had pioneered the style back in Paris in the middle of the nineteenth century: Ted had come across it purely by chance. Or possibly fate.

Mike and Ted became, for a while, inseperable surf buddies. They scored heroic, spectacular and occasionally devastating waves on the far-flung shores of Wales and the West Country. Mike now lives in Nelson, New Zealand, the opposite end of the world to England, where he had started out. To get there you have to fly in to Wellington, at the south end of the North Island, then hire a car, take the ferry across the Cook Strait to the South Island and then drive two or three hours up, down and around the vertiginous mountains. In darkness. Potentially getting a flat tyre on the way. Which pretty much covers my journey. Mike held the key to Ted's early surfing days back in England, after his return from the

West Coast. From Mike's house, in the daylight, you can see out across the break known as Snapper Rocks. And you can see the "tepee" on the beach that Mike has created out of driftwood and stones. Stray people shelter in there from the elements and leave grateful messages in the visitors' book. Mike's first wife died young in a car smash and now he is married to Rhonda, who fed me when I finally got there, close to midnight, still dizzy from the drive, and served up a mug of her homemade kombucha.

"He was the only kid with green hair," said Mike, fondly. He still loved Ted and was grieved to hear about how he died. But he had no illusions about his old school friend. He knew exactly how torn up he was, "damaged," by everything that had happened to him. Now over sixty (the age Ted would be if he were still alive), Mike looks lithe and fit and makes sixty look like it's still youthful and brimming over with health and enthusiasm. He once directed his own dance company and is now a sponsored bodysurfer (Slyde Handboards, San Diego) and a certified personal trainer, in yoga and dance and martial arts. He gives classes at the CityFitness gym in Nelson, but is also peripatetic, going out and about to help those who cannot make it in to the gym, on account of some disability or condition. I had the feeling that if I could only stick around long enough he would get me as supple as a good surfer ought to be. He is driven by a burning desire to fix everyone who needs fixing. And he is still trying to fix Ted, even though it's twenty years too late.

They were both landlocked surfers. Mike drew pictures of "Aqua Elves" (based on Tolkien), which is how they saw themselves: long-haired, adventurous, virtuous. There was one picture of the Elves hanging out of a VW camper van with surfboards strapped on top. Ted and Mike used to go surfing together back then in odd, far-flung places in the west of England or Wales, fringing the Atlantic, chauffeured by Ted's father. Bill was driving an old Rolls Royce. "I think it was a Phantom. Black. The size of a small ship. With a drinks cabinet in the back. Everything in there smelled of polish and leather. And there was a walnut dashboard." It was like a throwback to another age–of ease and comfort and unlimited affluence. The car was so big that they could just throw their boards and wetsuits in the back. They put towels on the seats to protect them.

"One weekend we drove to a spot next to the steelworks in Port Talbot. It was totally polluted. Dead pigs, empty bottles. It was dismal, horrible. The beach was black with grime. And the waves were pathetic. But we loved every second of it anyway." They were playing hooky from school, after all, they were escaping from all duties and responsibilities. It felt like freedom. Ted was the better surfer of the two and Mike always respected that, just as Ted, in return, appreciated Mike's artwork and ability on the harmonica.

This was a time when Bill was trying to placate Ted, to win him over, to make him see that he could stay in England and be the next Earl of Coventry, sit in the House of Lords and all that, and still do what he loved to do. There was no incompatibility. Maybe they could be friends? Surely it was not too late? But Ted remained as rebellious as ever. He refused to be reconciled. When they went back to Earls Croome, Ted would always turn his record player up loud, and leave the door open, so it echoed through the house. Bob

Dylan, the Eagles, the Grateful Dead, Led Zeppelin, Pink Floyd: Ted was fairly sure that Bill would hate all of them.

Bill tried hard not to say anything though. Gritted the teeth. He wanted Ted to feel at home here, he had enough restrictions at school.

But Ted carried on feeling disgruntled anyway. So what if there was a butler with white gloves and portraits of Coventrys of yore on the oak-panelled walls? Had he not been torn away from his beloved West Coast and mother and dumped in the middle of England? He didn't belong here. He refused to belong. In one part of his psyche, he always felt as if he'd been kidnapped by pirates and was being held hostage (even while enjoying some of the benefits of the British ruling class and riding around in a Rolls Royce). According to Mike there was one track in particular that he would play over and over: the Doobie Brothers, "Long Train Running," featuring lots of heavy guitars, a relentless pulse and the haunting refrain, "Without love where would you be now?"

"That was pure Ted," says Mike. "Listen to it." He played it for me on his computer. There was a line about a woman who "lost her home and her family" and how she wouldn't be going back. "You see, Ted lost his home and his family—or he felt he had, which amounts to the same thing—and he needed to replace them." He tended to think of Bill as more of an uncle figure, benevolent or otherwise. A distant relative of some kind. Technically family, but not close to his heart. Part-pirate and hostage taker. "He didn't understand about being differentiated," says Mike.

By "differentiated" Mike meant having a strong sense of self. Ted was always fluid, floating, betwixt and between, neither one thing nor another, and therefore was always drawn to those who were differentiated, solidly anchored in their own identity. Substitute father figures. Perhaps he had, as someone suggested, a "negative ego." Uprooted from England and transplanted to Los Angeles, then wrenched right back again, Ted felt unmoored, all at sea, in search of some kind of ratification or recognition. And never quite getting enough. Maybe he never would. "He repeated the same thing again and again," says Mike. "It was always *Groundhog Day* with Ted."

He mentions a couple of classic Ted dramas by way of explanation.

One time Mike and Ted were staying on a farm near one of their surf spots in Devon in the southwest of England. The farmer's daughter fell in love with Mike. Mike was seventeen, she—rosy-cheeked with freckles—was fifteen. Or if not love, a major crush. A passion. She had eyes only for Mike. Which is what caused the problem with Ted. Ted and Mike didn't look too dissimilar: both had long hair, parted in the middle, with a hint of Jesus about them. Ted was her age but she preferred the older guy. "It was a hopeless love that didn't go anywhere," says Mike. "But it was excruciating for Ted. He felt left out."

What really drove Ted to distraction was that Mike did absolutely nothing to respond to the farmer's daughter. Mike was shy and uncertain and unwilling to get involved. Which seemed like madness to Ted. Ted was willing but she was indifferent; she loved Mike but he was oblivious. A very imperfect triangle. The injustice and asymmetry of it infuriated Ted. He was jealous of Mike, but also irritated by his cool detachment. She was beautiful and he was ignoring her. It was virtually an insult. Ted wanted to grab Mike and shake some sense into him. But then their time at the farm was up and they had to troop off to the station and take the train back to school.

So they were walking down the street together, good mates again, when the rosy-cheeked farm girl came running down the street after them. "How could you leave without coming to say goodbye to me?" she moaned, and wrapped herself around Mike in an enveloping hug, planting a big kiss right on his lips, before running back to the farm. Ted was "in a sulk" all the way back to school. Crushed. Almost as if he didn't exist. The invisible man. Mike was clearly the chosen one. Even though nothing had really happened.

Another time they were surfing in Croyde together. On the surf-rich north shore of Devon, Croyde, on its day, could be the best surf spot in the whole of the British Isles. And this was one of those days. Perfect blue sky, perfect waves, between six and eight feet, vertical, tubular and neatly groomed by an offshore breeze. Verging on epic. In fact it was epic, as epic as it was ever likely to get in England in the middle of summer. This was the focal point for surfing in Britain, pulling in people from far and wide. There were even a few standout Australian surfers in action. Not only that but a reputable filmmaker had chosen this particular day to come and film the surfing at Croyde. Including Ted. Ted, then aged sixteen, surfed some of the best waves of his young life. It was like he could do no wrong. They were dream waves. Every wave he dropped into turned into a spectacular tube. All his best moves collected together in one spot on one day, like a stamp album containing only the rarest and most collectible stamps. The sun was shining and the cameras were rolling. He was in his element and his West Coast experience surely gave him an edge over the locals. He was not pushy or greedy where the waves were concerned, he didn't have to take every one, but he was quietly confident that he would stand out from the crowd and that his superior skills and style would be duly noted and recognized and exhibited by the filmmaker. Finally, justice had been done, Ted assumed.

The film was shown at a makeshift pop-up cinema on the beach a week later. A drive-in at the beach. A Saturday night. A big crowd from all around. People sitting on deckchairs or towels or just sprawling on the sand. The film rolls. The sun is there. The perfect blue sky is there. The perfect blue waves are there. Ted is there. The proof, on celluloid, that he really exists and is worthy of life. Recognition by the rest of mankind, even if only in a small way. But, as it turns out, rather smaller than he had anticipated. He must have made at least a dozen or more outstanding, meritorious, highly photogenic waves. For one reason or another, nearly all of them ended up on the cutting room floor. One alone put in an appearance, and you could just about make out it was Ted all right, if you already knew him, but it was sort of distant and a little bit shaky, so you had to know how it had gone down and then you could replay it in your head, which is what Ted did. He was part of it, but he was marginal.

But again, for reasons unknown and presumably it was sheer bad luck, the ride of the day, the most superlative and archetypal tube ride—as far as the film was concerned and therefore the audience watching the film—went to one "Panda" (real name Andy Marks). A mild-mannered local who happened to be a good friend of Mike's and was somewhere around the top of the tree at Croyde. His ride seemed to go on forever. He was a "goofy" (right foot to the front of the board) and so rode the wave backhand. And the filmmaker covered it from a couple of angles too. As the lens zoomed in on the ecstatic face of Panda, cries of enthusiasm went up from the assembled masses. "Go, Panda!" and "Yay, Panda!" And it swelled to become like a chant: "Pan-da! Pan-da! Pan-da!" There was shrieking and whistling and cheering. There was no question about it, Panda was the star of the night. From Ted's point of view, Panda was living the dream right there–not just surfing the perfect wave but, moreover, it being understood among the public at large that this was exactly what he was doing and therefore receiving benediction a second time around. Unless you received the endorsement of the filmmaker and audience it was almost as if your wave didn't exist, as if you didn't exist. Panda existed.

But Panda himself didn't necessarily appreciate what a big deal that was. He didn't much need approbation and vindication. Not in the way that Ted did. He was one of those lucky "differentiated" types, with the rock solid sense of self, and no doubts about his own existence and place in the universe. He didn't even take surfing that seriously. He was more into painting, if anything, and was preoccupied by a canvas he was working on. This is what Ted heard when, by chance, they happened to be walking down the road later that night, just the two of them, with the film over and the crowds all dispersed. Although in his heart of hearts fundamentally jealous, Ted had been pleased for Panda. Panda had what he, Ted, dreamed of. The adulation of the masses. And must therefore be elated. But rather as in the case of Mike and the rosy-cheeked farm girl, he (Panda) didn't fully appreciate how huge it was and how he should be basking in the glory of it. It was, in short, wasted on him.

So Ted was congratulating him, as they went along the barely lit street around midnight, and Panda, on the other hand, was saying stuff like, "Ha! It was nothing," and "I guess it was just a lucky shot." He wasn't even being modest. He really did think it was nothing. That was what annoyed Ted. Whereas it was not nothing, it was something, something of immense if hard-to-define significance. And meanwhile here was this numskull who didn't even realize how massive it really was.

Which is when Ted hit him. He couldn't help it. The guy needed it, just to wake him up. Ted pulled his fist back and hit him on the right side of the face with a roundhouse punch. Not powerful, but completely out of the blue, and enough to deck him. Panda went down, crumpled to his knees. Dazed, he looked back up at Ted with a questioning look. He was more mystified than anything else. What the hell was that about? How had this perfectly polite young guy with blonde hair and the American accent turned into a psycho? Panda wondered if Ted was going to finish him off and give him a good kicking too, now he was down.

But Ted was horrified at what he had done. He didn't know how and why he had turned into a maniac. He looked at his own clenched fist and was just as mystified as Panda, and mortified into the bargain. This was not appropriate behavior for an Aqua Elf, surely? So he did the only thing he could do in the circumstances: he ran. He ran and kept on running all the way back to the beach and dived into the sea in the darkness and swam underwater until his lungs were on fire.

The next day he sought out Panda and apologized profusely and Panda, who had a purple bruise on the side of his head where Ted had hit him, was all forgiveness. Which was almost as annoying as his indifference to acclaim. "It took Ted months to recover," Mike says, "he used to beat himself up about it." That was the redeeming thing about Ted: he behaved badly but at least he felt guilty about it afterwards and owned up.

"He needed approval from everyone around him," Mike says. "Which he got, mostly. But he would overdo it and therefore blow it." He could never quite get enough recognition to fill the aching, yawning gap that lurked within, to quell the scintillating self-doubt. Mike and Ted were at Millfield School together for a year or so. It was one of the most "progressive" schools in England. Co-ed, liberal, verging on permissive. Near Glastonbury with something of the rock festival vibe, with sons of sultans and daughters of movie stars and scholarships for the less affluent. And a certain amount of drug-taking, mostly cannabis. Mike earned a place there by virtue of (a) having been born in a mangrove swamp in Malaysia and (b) when he was interviewed in the headmaster's study, being able to name all the species of ducks in the duck pond. They took Ted to add to the diversity of species among the students.

Mike was a regular at a school club which attracted all the school intellectuals, where they would smoke their pipes and discuss existentialism and Camus and Dostoyevsky.

Ted went along but he never really felt part of it, largely on account of not doing the reading. He insisted that Mike read *The Lord of the Rings*. He had a soft spot for tales of daring and heroism and extreme villainy, whether real or imaginary. I can't help but wonder, though, if he might have enjoyed *The Brothers Karamazov*, which is all about bumping off your own father. Or *The Outsider*.

Ted dropped out of school while Mike was in his final year. "He never really took to it," Mike says. "He wanted to belong and he never did." Mike went to art college and started building Lakota tepees, living in one with his artist girlfriend Ges Wilson (who did all the stitching) for a few years and Ted would come to stay with them, pitching his tent next to their tepee. Then Mike got a job as a teacher, went on an exchange year to New Zealand, fell in love with the place and never returned.

12.

"Ted lacked the power of now," Carolyn said. A phrase that has stuck in my mind.

But there was surely a reason for that. For one thing Ted was still living in England at the time. Theoretically he was now studying at Dartington Hall, a "progressive co-ed" in the west country. Kind of an art college. Leafy thousand-acre estate. Inspired by John Dewey, American pragmatist philosopher. No rewards, no penalties, just do it, if you feel in the mood. "No one knew anyone who did any work there," said one of Ted's contemporaries, Phil Holden, the photographer. According to its prospectus, there was to be "no corporal punishment, indeed no punishment at all; no prefects; no uniforms; no Officers' Training Corps; no segregation of the sexes; no compulsory games, compulsory religion or compulsory anything else, no more Latin, no more Greek; no competition; no jingoism." No one was sure what was to take their place. Maybe more painting, more music, symphonies and swimming and sonnets. One guy took an entire VW van apart and put it back together again—but on the roof of the school, where it would remain for years to come. Ted was doing research on surfboard design.

Which somehow led me to PJ. PJ and Ted had chased waves together around the world, in South Africa and Hawaii and Australia. They had represented Great Britain together. I still owe PJ £10. I didn't have enough to pay the taxi when I got out at Llangennith right outside PJ's Surf Shop way out west on the Gower Peninsula. PJ donated the tenner in the name of Ted. "He sort of wanted to be me," he said. "Or Nigel." PJ was European champion and Welsh national champion at the time, and Nigel Semmens was the champion of England. Ted, aged seventeen, was still up-and-coming. "He wasn't right up there," said PJ, "but he was very energized. Emotional. I could feel the love coming off him towards me."

So emotional, in fact, that he had once had a fight with another guy inside a car when the guy dared to doubt whether or not he was going to make it at the highest level. It hadn't gone that well. Ted was driving at the time and he only had one arm free. But, come what may, he would fight back, he would not give up. He was driving an old banger at the time, a brown builder's van with his surfboards strapped to the top. He drove around the country in it, from contest to contest, always on the lookout for fresh waves to surf. Sometimes he would stay at a castle owned by his uncle on the Pembrokeshire coast. He even got to surf "Oxwich Point," a far-flung rarity of a wave that almost never worked but was perfect when it did. "I missed out," said PJ, "but Ted was on it. When it was firing. He was so lucky."

There were a lot of people in PJ's Surf Shop when I was there, clamoring for boards or wax or whatever, mostly being seen to by his wife or daughter. One of them came up to PJ and called him a "legend." PJ said, "I hate the word 'legend'– at least until you die, then you're welcome to use it."

"I guess we can call Ted a legend then," I said.

PJ–Pete Jones–laughed. "He always was a legend. Even when he was alive. The bigger the waves the better he got." PJ and Ted trooped around together a lot back then. PJ had long hair and a big bushy moustache and he rode a board with no leash, in classic style, even on big days. The leash would just get in his way. Rather like an umbilical cord. It happened that Ted was present at the birth of PJ's son in October 1977. Or rather, they both sort of missed it. They were driving together in Ted's van when PJ got the call from the hospital. They were coming back from Freshwater West where PJ had just won the Welsh title. Ted came fourth. Ted offered him a lift back to Swansea. PJ hopped in and put his boards on the roof. They drove off and the ancient vehicle duly broke down somewhere in the back of beyond. Lost in Wales. On a Sunday afternoon. They finally got towed to a garage that repaired the vehicle on the Monday, and then drove off to the maternity ward. Ted was standing right there when PJ saw his son James for the very first time. James was born on the 1st, they got there on the 2nd, it could have been worse.

It was a bond between them, but also the parting of the ways. PJ realized that if he wanted to do what Ted was doing–in effect, surfing the entire world in search of an elusive crown–then he wouldn't be able to live in Britain any more. And he would have to leave wife and child behind. So he decided, on this very day, to give up competitive surfing and open his surf shop instead. He didn't want to be forever on the road, breaking down and missing birthdays. "I had the surfing feeling whether I was right here or somewhere else." When they were in South Africa together, at the 1978 World Amateur championships, held at Nahoon Reef, East London,

PJ—captain of the GB team—effectively passed on the baton to Ted: "I'm too old, Ted boyo," he said over a beer, "but you really should turn pro, it's what you've always wanted."

PJ recalled one incident in Hawaii, sometime in the late seventies, that might have also influenced his decision to retire, on top of being a young dad. He was out at Kammieland, the smaller break adjacent to Sunset where Ted preferred to surf. PJ was surfing on his own. Which was his mistake. He should have had a team around him. It was a sunny morning, the water was glassy, the waves were easy, everything looked set fair, but PJ soon found himself surrounded by five grouchy Hawaiians. All of them big guys. PJ was not a big guy. More slim and svelte and balletic, only with a lot of hair. Which was not going to give him that much protection in the current context. They sat there on their boards, all around PJ, like Cherokees around a wagon train. They had their arms folded. Almost as if they were throwing up a barrier, a customs barrier, in a small nation that resented outsiders. "Who the fuck are you?" said one of them to PJ. "And where the fuck you from?" said another.

PJ tried to explain. "Where the fuck is Wales?" they said. They had a notion it could be connected to New South Wales i.e. Australia i.e. they were going to inflict some serious punishment on this haole interloper. "If I'd said Australia they would have ripped into me right there." Hawaiians had it in for all Australians during this period. PJ had to use hand signals to explain exactly where Wales was in relation to England. The extreme west coast of Britain, sticking out in the direction of Ireland. Scotland up here, Cornwall down there. Wales, you see, this bit in the middle, to the left. The

Hawaiians didn't like the sound of it but they were a little bit mystified by the geography so they paddled off again to find someone else to hassle. "The aloha had long gone," said PJ.

Then he thought about Ted in Hawaii. "Ted wasn't mean enough in the water. It's almost like being in the boxing ring. You have to want to really hurt the other guy, take his head off. I had that when I was young. My ego kicked in. Ted didn't have that. He had a lot of love for other surfers. Maybe you have to lose that."

PJ had a mystical side to him, partly on account of one or two near misses in his life. One time he was drowning (having been hit on the head by someone's board–he still has the scars) and all he could see was "white light." Jesus Christ, he argued, was pure white light, "and he was the first stand-up paddle boarder too." But PJ reckoned that when it came to contests, you needed your share of "black light." Pure black light was when you wanted to kill someone, or terrorism. People have both, but in a contest (says PJ) you should "feel the white light" but at the same time "a bit of black light comes in."

"Ted had plenty of white light," PJ said. Not enough black.

His wife Carolyn drove me back to the station. "The white light streamed out of her eyes," PJ said of her. So we were talking about her memories of Ted. Which is when she came out with her line about Ted lacking "the power of now." She was an aficionado–almost a disciple, you might say–of Eckhart Tolle, author of the book *The Power of Now* (which I had read, so I recognised the allusion). A guide to "spiritual enlightenment." She was going to a Tolle lecture in London later in the year too. A long long way from Llangennith, so she was serious. The whole point of Tolle was the importance of the present, living in the moment, being there (*Dasein*, Heidegger would say) and appreciating and savoring the strangeness and the beauty of transience. If you were drinking a cup of coffee you had to do nothing but taste the coffee, concentrate fully on the essence of the bean. If you were surfing then you would do nothing but surf. You would be, in fact, the Surfer and nothing else (not, for example, shall we say, an accountant who happened to be going surfing for the day). It was one man on a board on a wave, that particular man on just that board on just this wave, no more and no less. A perfect fusion of body and mind and existence. In theory.

My train pulled away from the little Welsh station, going east, to the right in PJ's terms, back in the general direction of England.

PJ had the power of now. He had been invited off to Narabeen in Australia, but he didn't go. "I'll only know a few guys. And I'll only get one wave. Whereas here I can get all the waves I want and I know everyone. I don't mind if it's two foot. It's paradise in itself." Ted wasn't like that. Carolyn was right. He was always dreaming, never fully satisfied. Everything was an allegory for Ted, a symbol of something else. He did go off to Australia. He was never just a surfer: in his mind he was Winston Churchill or King Arthur too. On a mission or a quest. A man who would be king of the waves. Restless nomad that he was, wherever he was, he needed to be somewhere else. The present was a myth to Ted, like an imaginary point in space that didn't have any real existence. "He wasn't in the now, he was always striving forwards," Carolyn said. Forwards or backwards, I thought. Perhaps he was born in the wrong era. He couldn't live in the present, he lived in the past and the future, a lost realm of knights and ladies and that distant paradise in which he was surfing champion of the world. Which is when, on that miraculous day, he would acquire the power, single-handedly, to usher in the new wave of the True, the Good and the Beautiful.

Until then he would just have to keep wielding his trusty sword, his Excalibur, his surfboard.

13

"Deya," Ted's letter began. (Technically that should read *Deya'*, but he left out the diacritical mark: her name means "Eternal Light.") Ted and Deya' were students together at Dartington Hall. Co-ed, no segregation. She was in the year below him. Ted was in love. He wrote the following letter from Hawaii (full and unexpurgated), circa 1975:

> Tonight is the night before Xmas–not much like winter because I'm suffering from a sunburn right now. Today the surf was about 15–20 foot and too stormy to surf. Up till now I haven't told you much about Hawaii, so I'll tell you. The beaches are unreal, you could live in paradise if you could get away from the tourists. The sands are white and made from sea shells and coral. Palm trees are every[where] and the cliffs are green, the water is turquoise on calm days. The fish are full[-]on rainbows.
>
> Lots of beautiful blondes around, but as I'm not winning the big prize money contests right now I don't see to[o] much of them. I know and surf with most of the people I used to have on my wall.
>
> Anyway I would be unreal stoked if you can keep your extravagant promise and come and live with me, believe it or not I think about you a lot and all the mistakes I made, I'd probably make the same mistikes [sic] if I did it all over again.
>
> In a few days I'm moving again, so I'll send Dave and Wendy my new address in a few weeks, ok. Thanks for the photo it brings back a few happy memories.

Take care of yourself,
Love
Ted
PS how come you never let yourself go–hell knows I tried enough.
PPS when I'm rich I'll send you a gift worthy of 3,000 miles and you.

On her father's side, Deya' was related to Jesse James. Her mother was a Palestinian. She was born in Boston, raised in Beirut, and ended up studying for A-levels (English, history and jewellery-making) at Dartington Hall. "We were all refugees and rejects," she said. She and Ted alike. And they both had an American parent. She was known as "Deya' the American."

I met her in the winter of 2017 at a Pain Quotidien on the East Side in New York and we went to the UN together for a Palestinian Solidarity Day. She had been a model, had married a man who died the same year as Ted, and was now working for an international educational charity. "Was he always such a loner?" she wanted to know.

I even bumped into her father at the UN and he said that when he had been to visit Dartington Hall once he was struck that there were absolutely no adults around. It was a weekend and the place had been completely taken over by students. Anarchy reigned. It was like a drug-fuelled mass orgy (teachers reportedly slept with students too). With one exclusion. For Ted, it was no drugs, no sex (an abstinence only partly voluntary).

Deya' had been in touch with a girl (as she then was) who had been at the school and slept with every single boy she met. Except for Ted. No, she did not sleep with Ted, she explained. For the simple reason that he was too "needy." He was too hurt, too wounded. He cared too much. The words "desperate" and "traumatised" came to mind. And he wasn't a "druggie." Which meant that Ted did not belong to the "clique" composed of students who (a) took a lot of drugs (b) had been at the previous feeder school and (c) saw themselves as Masters of the Universe i.e. good-looking with money. Their "Queen Bitch" (as Deya' described her) wore a top hat. They once chained a boy they didn't like to a tree and he had to be rescued by the fire brigade. They were like the scary schoolkids in *Lord of the Flies,* the savagery barely concealed beneath a veneer of manners.

Ted had felt like he didn't belong at Millfield and now at Dartington he remained an outsider. More American than English. More hippy than punk. The same pattern repeating itself. Groundhog Day, as Mike Baker said. One time the clique invaded his room (there were no locks), had a party there, got drunk on cheap cider ("scrumpy") and trashed the place. Ted finally came back and furiously threw them all out. "He wanted to behave well, but they didn't." Ted felt as if it was him versus everyone else: apart from Deya'. "We were both outsiders," she said.

Dartington Hall was not known for the rigor of its education. One young Casanova was expelled for giving everyone a venereal disease. Drugs were virtually obligatory, especially acid. One student died of a heroin overdose. Another died when he tried to take a piss standing on a window sill. But apparently Ted did indeed study. He even took a photography A-level. And he was quite serious about it too. Deya' was fairly sure he didn't actually get the A-level but he worked hard and spent hours in the dark room developing his photos. Most of the photos in the personal "year book" that Deya' showed me are taken by Ted (thus Ted is never seen in any of them—this is the pre-selfie era). When Ted speaks of his "mistakes" in his letter (or "mistikes") he is probably not talking about photography, however.

It happened on another weekend, around New Year. Ted and a crew from Dartington Hall went to Earls Croome together in his van. With the emphasis on "party." Again, no grown-ups. Bill was away and the staff had the weekend off. They had the place to themselves and they could do whatever they liked. Deya' recalled that, in the great formal dining room, oak panelled and adorned with ancestral portraits, they had dinner quite literally *under* the table. "We were all so fucked-up." High on pot.

Deya' was assigned a four-poster bed in the bedroom next to Ted's. Which was not a coincidence. That evening, New Year's Eve, Ted asked her flat out, "Can you come and sleep in my room?" She was mopping up a flood from the dishwasher at the time (she'd never used one before and had just squirted in Fairy Liquid). "Sorry, Ted," she said. "I've got my boyfriend coming. He is staying in my room."

Ted was crestfallen. The fact is that she had only just dumped Kent, the previous boyfriend. Ted had assumed there was a vacancy. He had politely waited for the right opportunity to pledge his troth. But before he could turn around, another guy, name of Marco, who looked like Mick Jagger, had stepped in to fill the temporary vacuum. And the new boyfriend duly turned up. Ted was not too happy about it.

"Pissed off," says Deya'. Ted had no idea Marco was coming. You just couldn't stop this guy! Or could you . . . ?

Deya' and Marco have sex. Enthusiastically. Possibly all through the night. There is a possibility also that Ted overhears the sounds of orgasmic frenzy all night long. Ted was a sensitive guy. I am calling it "extenuating circumstances," because it might help to explain if not entirely justify what happened next.

Ted brings them coffee the following morning. "You didn't need to do that," says Deya'.

"It comes as standard with B & B." He leaves the coffees and goes out again.

"Nice guy," says Marco, who, within the hour, is having his stomach pumped at the local hospital. He survives.

Nobody died. But you might call it, if pushed, "attempted homicide." Because Ted–he owned up later–had stirred a little rat poison into Marco's coffee. Only Ted could imagine that he would kill off the boyfriend and then he and Deya' would get to ride off into the sunset together. Deya' says now that Ted "probably" didn't want to kill anyone, only make the guy "uncomfortable." We agree that it is hard to know just how much rat poison you need to put in a cup of coffee to have the required effect.

But remember, it was "mistikes" plural. This was only one among many, if perhaps the most extreme. Deya' became one of his best friends at Dartington Hall. She would go to the beach with him and watch him surfing. His token beach babe. He had once said to her, in one of his fits of melancholy, "Why don't other people do the things I like to do? I'm always doing what they like to do." Ted had locked into a pursuit that was by definition marginal and eccentric and counter-cultural, and yet he wanted to be accepted all the same. But it was a line that resonated with Deya'. "I realised he was feeling sad and neglected." So she would often hang out with Ted when no one else would. Which was half great for Ted, half torture (because she would never go to bed with him–they kissed once, but that was it–a consummation devoutly to be wished). Maybe it is not so surprising that she got to play the part of Claudius at school in a performance of *Hamlet* (i.e. she is the guy who kills the king–Hamlet's father–by pouring a vial of leperous distilment in his ear).

But Ted had another habit Deya' found annoying. She would keep him company working in the darkroom for hours on end. Then they would walk back to their dorm through a graveyard. Every time, Ted insisted on hiding behind a grave-stone or sepulchre and jumping out screaming and wailing like some monstrous evil spirit. Terrifying in the darkness. Every time she would tell him she didn't like it and it scared her. And still he would keep on doing it. Never giving up. Persisting. Even when he knew he shouldn't. Locked into a pattern of behavior that he could never quite shake. "He would always push too far," Deya' said. "He didn't know how to behave."

Another time he held a knife to her throat. "It was only a butter knife," she said. But still. Ted had rushed into the student dorm, where the clique was holding court, pretending to be having a bad trip (he had neither good nor bad ones), arms flapping around, with coffee drooling out of his mouth. And had duly set upon her (dressed, she said, "like a Spanish hooker"), held the knife to her throat, and kidnapped her. In a spirit of jest. A hilarious practical joke. Which, alas, nobody found that funny, not even the ones who were high as kites. Deya' had a theory: "Ted really wanted to be rejected. His perfect woman was the one who would say no."

Towards the end of his time at Dartington Hall, the headmaster–known to all as "John," for once actually on the premises and sitting in the headmaster's study–made a recommendation to Ted. It was an idea that had never occurred to him before. But it made perfect sense to his mind. "You could always major in surfing at the University of Hawaii," he said.

He was probably being ironic. But it planted the seed.

14.

It is often said of the top pros that "he could surf an ironing board, and he would still look good." Or words to that effect. Ted would not agree. The board had to be just right. In his mind, there was such a thing as "the magic board," just as there was a magic sword, Excalibur, and a magic ring in *Lord of the Rings*. This board would make whoever rode it into a god, all-seeing and all-surfing. Infallible. Omnipotent. This, after all, was the subject of his studies (such as they were) at Dartington Hall. So it was that he sought out the advice and inspiration of others. Even in England, he was always in search of a guru.

In the 1970s, North Devon became, as the British Surfing Museum nicely put it, "a hotbed of surfing design and innovation." Ted sought out the shapers of repute, rather like a young D'Artagnan riding off to join forces with the Musketeers. Among them were many young Australians. I received the following message from Kevin Cross, an Australian who had set up a board-shaping business ("cutting edge" declares the British Surfing Museum) in Braunton, a town in Devon close to Croyde, Ted's break of choice. Ted would have been around sixteen at the time.

MEETING TED DEERHURST

In the early '70s I was making surfboards in Braunton, North Devon using my label "Creamed Honey Surfboards." I was in the shaping bay one day when Linda walked in to say there was a young guy with his father in the showroom who would like to talk to me about a surfboard.

I walked out to meet this guy; he was young, had blond hair and talked with an American accent. He introduced himself as Ted. He told me he had just returned to the UK and would like me to make him a new board. I was struck by his passion and enthusiasm for surfing and his energy for life.

After some discussion about the type of board he would like, I was aware that Ted had very strong ideas on exactly what he wanted, and asked if he could be in the shaping bay with me when it was shaped.

The next day, Ted arrived and we started on his board. After lengthy discussions about plan-shape, bottom, deck, rail type and thickness, I added some suggestions, based on local knowledge about the types of waves he would be surfing. Many hours later with Ted keeping a very close eye on proceedings, the board was finished.

I must admit I was pleased with the end result.

Ted explained how he wanted the board glassed and the design he would like, and off he went with his father, happy in the knowledge the board would be ready to collect the next weekend. I finished the board and it looked great.

When Ted arrived to collect the board, he bounced into the factory with all the enthusiasm and excitement I would later come to know and expect from Ted.

I did suggest that it would be best if he gave it a week to cure before taking it in the water . . . I knew that was never going to happen.

Ted was impatient to go but waited for his dad to write the cheque, then almost ran out to the street with his new board. I walked out with his father and we had a brief discussion about Ted's passion for surfing.

When we arrived at the car, I found Ted pushing his board into the back seat of a large black limo, and off they went, straight to the beach.

Walking back into the factory I decided to look at the check. It was then I found Ted's father was the Earl of Coventry and Ted a Viscount.

Not once in all the years I knew Ted did he ever use his status or title to gain favour in anything he did.

After finishing work in the factory for that day, I went straight to Croyde beach for a surf. I paddled out to find Ted still in the water, as I expected, with the biggest smile on his face. He was full of excitement about his new board and could not stop chatting about what a great surf he was having. His surfing ability and knowledge was at a very high level. That was a great day.

For the many years I knew Ted, he just continued to follow his passion of surfing, making his own surfboards and becoming a professional surfer on the world circuit.

In the process he became, and still is, a Legend of British Surf History and an all-round great guy.

Kevin Cross

Maybe, at least for a moment, Ted had found his magic board.

"Linda" in this account, is Linda Nash, who was then Mrs Cross. Owing to some strange interweaving of destinies, she is now living in Earls Croome and has recently signed up as a National Trust volunteer at Croome Court itself, where Ted's family had its seat for generations. She carries a vivid memory of Ted around with her like a lucky charm bracelet. She saw him at Creamed Honey every day over a couple of weeks. Playing hooky from school, probably: or perhaps this was part of his "project"–under the broad heading of history and philosophy–*A Dissertation on the Theory and Practice of Board Design*. "He was a gorgeous-looking lad," she recalls. "Charming in every way. If I hadn't already been married, I would have married him like a shot." He looked like a young movie matinée idol. How could she not feel this way? "I could have fallen head over heels." Her girlfriends were also "sweet on him." Everyone fell for young Ted, so good-looking and yet so wounded. And no mother? He would need a lot of mothering, that was clear.

Linda remembers that Bill was "tall and imposing." When he paid, she had to go and ask him for a cheque guarantee card. "When I looked at the check with his name on–and the title, Earl or Lord–I wanted the earth to open and swallow me up. I felt awful." You don't ask 007 for a cheque guarantee card. A few years later the Creamed Honey factory burned down. Linda went on to become a make-up artist in Los Angeles, where she married an American (having first divorced Kevin), before returning here, to Croome, and Bill's graveside, in the little Saxon church adjacent to Croome Court. His favorite dog Nelson (among seven, five labradors and two shitzus) is buried across the street.

Bill let Ted throw his new board in the back of the Rolls. Can you really ask more of a father than that? Presumably Ted did. His quest for the perfect board continued. Which took him to an Aladdin's Cave outside Braunton. Paul "Blackie" Blacker had a genius for making things. He had a City and Guilds "distinction." He had worked on the Channel Tunnel at one point, reuniting the rogue island to the continent once more. And was once dug out of a concrete grave. Even while still serving his panel-beating apprenticeship, he had been headhunted by Aston Martin and invited to work on the construction of their James Bond-worthy sports cars in Birmingham. All handmade of course. He turned them down flat. "If I'd been offered a job with Rolls Royce I wouldn't have taken it," he said. He'd had enough of tunnels and car factories, he wanted to go and make surfboards in North Devon instead. But they were the Aston Martin or Rolls Royce of surfboards at that period, at least in England.

Blackie was a perfectionist. He was a "custom shaper," not a "production shaper," the surfing equivalent of a bespoke tailor. And Blackie's place in Braunton was the Savile Row of surfing. The great Greg Noll ("Da Bull"), fearless pioneer of Waimea Bay and Pipeline, was a fan. Naturally Ted knocked on his door one day and Blackie took him in and showed him the business. "The quality of your boards is supreme," Ted concluded. He was a perfectionist too. But with a mystical twist: In the beginning was the board and the board was with God and the board was God.

Ted would hang out with Blackie during the day and go and work as a "glass collector" at RUDA, a holiday camp in Croyde, by night. Blackie was built like a blacksmith of old, with arms like anvils, and he must have towered over the slightly built young Ted. He schooled Ted, in sanding and glassing and finishing, the wet and the dry polish, initiated him into the arcane mysteries of thickness and rocker and rail. Shortboards, longboards, round nose, pointed, one-fin, two, three even four: they were always striving after the perfect board, the one board that would be infallible. The True, the Good and the Beautiful, all rolled up into one solid piece of foam and glass fiber. Obviously Ted would have to pay his dues. One day he put his hand into a bucket of acetone and of course there had to be a Stanley knife in there. His hand was sliced open and the wound was ago- nisingly invaded by solvent. Ted fainted with the pain and had to be carried outside to recover. Another time he came up with the crazy idea, dismissed by unbelievers, of giving boards away for free.

At this time Blackie had taken over the Lightning Bolt franchise in Europe and many of his boards proudly wore the Lightning Bolt insignia. "All the pros were riding Lightning Bolts in Hawaii," said Blackie. Ted fell in love with Lightning Bolt. He loved the notion of energy pulsating through him, as if gifted by the gods. And the idea that it would enable him to conquer Hawaii. There came a moment, Blackie recalled, when Ted got the coveted Lightning Bolt sponsorship. In the short film script he would eventually write "based on the life of the British Lion, Lord Ted Deerhurst, professional surfer," the Ted-character has dinner in Honolulu with the Bolt corporation executives and then rushes out and announces ("really exuberant") to MR (Mark Richards–world champion from Australia), "I think I'm getting somewhere!"

It really was something like that in all probability. Henceforth Ted would have not only free boards, but also the right to make boards himself in the name of Lightning Bolt. And he was now part of a team that included the very stylish Gerry Lopez, aka "Mr Pipeline" and Jack Shipley, head judge of pro surfing. Ted thought he had it made then. Problem solved. He shaped one Lightning Bolt (yellow swallowtail tri-fin, six foot four inches, with extra rocker) for a local kid, Tim Barrow, then only fourteen, that was so good that he, Tim, instantly became Ted's protégé and disciple. Tim was the one and only soul I came across on my travels who said he wanted "to be like Ted." Ted was his Pied Piper and eventually led him off a few years later as far as Hawaii (in the teeth of protests from his accountant father and schoolteacher mother) and a huge day at Haleiwa. "He was serious," said Barrow, who would eventually dedicate himself to photography. "And he saw the potential in me."

Ted never stopped shaping. He shaped when he moved to Burleigh Heads, Australia, where he learned from MR. He shaped in Hawaii, where he learned from Randy Rarick, who gave him some of his templates. Bernie Baker reckoned Ted always preferred the roundtail over squashtails and pintails, "because it holds better in bigger waves. He was ambitious, always looking for an edge." When I met Ted in Hawaii in the winter of '89, I, like him, was still searching for the perfect board, still looking for that edge. I had bought a couple over the ages and I never thought they were quite right. (That "radical intermediate tri-fin," bought in Coogee Beach in 1982, turned out to be more like a lead weight around my ankle.) So Ted says to me, "You can have one of mine. Come on over."

It was like Father Christmas had landed on the North Shore. It was just what I needed, the answer to my prayers. I went over to Crazy Joe's Plantation Village and found him surrounded by an array of boards, all shapes and sizes, from a seven-foot thruster to an eleven-foot-long elephant gun, as if it had been raining boards recently. He picked one out for me from his quiver. By then, at the end of the eighties, it was an Excalibur, with the image of the sword running the length of the board, divided like a shield into green and purple quadrants. A big wave gun, long and slim and narrow in the tail. I was riding an Excalibur! I too was King Arthur. I too had a shot at the Holy Grail. Ted was now my shaper. My shaman.

I took that board out at Sunset, at Velzyland, and Haleiwa, and came a cropper in all three places. I just couldn't seem to get that board going. Eventually I went back to Ted, wounded (with bruises to the head and a gash on one knee) for further instruction. I assumed I must be doing something wrong. Maybe it was designed for a goofy-footer?

"I'm not surprised it didn't go well for you," he said.

"Really?"

"That board was one of my rejects. Must have been jinxed. Never worked for me either."

I said nothing, but my face must have shown a degree of disappointment. Father Christmas had given me a dud. I had been sunk by my own saviour. The Holy Grail postponed. Ted noticed that one of the fins was hanging loose–the casualty of one reef or another. "Don't worry," he said, tossing the board aside and putting a hand on my shoulder, perhaps recognising something of his experience in mine. "That was an apprentice work. I'll shape you a better one next time. I have a theory…"

He was an artist, always dissatisfied with his previous works. And he was a scientist too, ever ready to put his theories to a rigorous test, even if he was using me as his guinea pig. But with that visionary gleam in his eye, he was more like some ancient alchemist, looking for the secret formula that would finally transform base metal into purest gold, a board that was shaped like a philosopher's stone.

15.

There are a number of crucial turning points in Ted's short life. Mostly involving waves. One that didn't come with an ocean and a beach attached was cocktails at the Palace in the summer of '78. Buckingham Palace. The London residence of the British royal family. Unless a tsunami came crashing up the Thames (as in my childhood dream), it was a long way from any kind of decent wave. Ted wasn't going to meet the Queen. His host at the Palace was Prince Charles, then thirty, a decade older than Ted, and patron to the British Surfing Association. Charles was (and still is, as of time of writing) next in line to the throne. Ted was somewhere much lower down the rankings (one source reckoned "60th," another "700th," another still maintained he simply had no chance). But still, there was an affinity, a faint sense of mutual recognition. There was also an odd connection between surfing and the royals.

Surfing has long been known (together with horse racing, the Queen's preference) as "the sport of kings." It acquired the tag because "he'enalu" was practised and privileged by Hawaiian royals over the centuries. Perhaps the best surfer got to be king. Certainly, the king got the best waves, even if he had to be carried down the beach and ushered into the water by courtiers and flunkies. And then have his exploits set down in verse (no doubt hyperbolic) by his personal surf bard or chanter. Princess Kaiulani contributed to the rise of surfing in England when she gave a demo off Brighton in the 1890s. Also in unbuttoned Victorian England, two work shy Hawaiian princes–David Kawananakoa and Jonah Kuhio Kalanianaole–took surfing north to Bridlington on the gale-lashed shores of Yorkshire. But, going in the other direction, British royals had dabbled in surfing in Hawaii. There is a grainy photo, dating from 1920, of the young Prince of Wales–who would become King Edward VIII and later abdicate to marry his American divorcee Wallis Simpson–surfing Waikiki under the eye of legendary Hawaiian surfer and Olympic gold medallist Duke Kahanomoku (himself named after a visiting British dignitary). Peter Robinson of the British Surfing Museum reckoned that it was the earliest picture ever of a Brit riding a wave.

So it was natural that another Prince of Wales, Charles, should become patron of the British Surfing Association. And therefore, in the summer of 1978, invite the GB surfing team, captained by PJ and featuring Ted, before they took ship to the World Cup in South Africa, to join him for drinks at the Palace. Ted and PJ had hired a silver-green Mercedes for the purpose. And a chauffeur. The gates of Buckingham Palace were guarded by sentries in red coats and bearskin hats, armed with rifles. It was a warm summer's evening and hundreds of tourists were staring through the railings hoping for a glimpse of the Queen. Then the gates swung open to let the silver green Mercedes through. Ted was inside the grounds of the palace. PJ thought they were probably mistaken for some visiting rock band. They all had long hair and droopy moustaches, vintage Magical Mystery Tour–style. And, for once, suits and ties. But Ted virtually belonged here. It was almost like going home for Ted. The long corridors and the portraits on the walls of obscure grandees of old all looked familiar to him. He felt as if he was in a dream of some kind. Or like he was going back in time.

Charles, exercising the privilege of princes, was ninety minutes late. Prince Phillip landed in a helicopter on the lawn outside. Ted, who normally preferred orange juice, found himself drinking a lot of sherry in a vast room lined with tapestries depicting epic battles and vertiginous romance–reminiscent of the Tapestry Room at Croome Court. Maybe he needed the stiffer drink. When His Royal Highness finally arrived, he apologised profusely and welcomed these "modern-day Neptunes" with a short speech, anticipating their imminent achievements on far-flung shores. Then he mingled with the members of the team and spoke to them individually.

Ted was standing with a fellow surfer, Graham Niles. Charles asked him if the lump on his head was caused by a surfboard hitting him. "Not exactly," Niles replied. It turned out that it was caused by his girlfriend when, for one reason or another, she hit him over the head with a telephone. Ted, on the face of it, appeared unscarred. He did, however, have an incipient moustache.

"I notice a lot of surfers have rather splendid moustaches," Charles said. "Is that to keep you warm in the water?" That got a good laugh.

Ted asked if the Prince ever went surfing himself. Charles replied that he had surfed in the past–at Constantine Bay in Cornwall (and there are pictures online to prove it too)–but that he was now officially retired and that he was therefore very glad that Ted (Viscount Edward Deerhurst, formally speaking) was surfing in his place, on behalf of the nation. In effect, standing in for Charles. A surrogate Prince, or future King. Ambassador or special envoy to Hawaii.

When they were leaving the Palace in the silver-green Mercedes, Ted may have said exactly what he said to me more than a decade later in Hawaii: "I don't understand how the dude can live in London all the time when he could go and live anywhere he likes." Prince Charles was next in line to be King; Ted was next in line to be the Earl of Coventry. But Prince Charles took his destiny seriously and thought of little else, even if the longevity of the Queen would force him to be patient. Whereas Ted, in contrast, had no ambition to become Earl. He did not want to sit in the House of Lords. He did not want to live in London. He was always a beach boy at heart. To him Buckingham Palace was a symbol of his servitude in England. He was glad to be heading for East London, South Africa, which at least had a beach and an ocean.

Ted preferred the sport of kings to any actual king.

16.

There are plenty of news clippings and interviews with Ted over the years, from all around the world. I can only offer a brief summary of some of the highlights. "Lord on a board" is a phrase that catches on. It gets Ted noticed, but it also becomes a monkey on his back. Almost a target. He can make the rare claim to have featured in a cover shot for *Surfer* and appeared in the Australian edition of *Playboy*.

1978, BRITAIN
"I simply want to be the best surfer in Britain, earning my keep from it and surfing for my country...The immediate drawback is that there are no professional surfers in Britain and Britain does not even have a surfing team."

Oct 16, 1979. Ted comes 5th in the Welsh open championships, despite surfing with an injury. He is then ranked 60th in world surfing "and he is confident about improving on that." The headline is "TED ALL SET FOR THE HIGHEST WAVE."

Also 1979: Ted is awarded "Surfer of the Year" in Britain (shared with Linda Sharp) by British Surf Magazine.

HAWAII, 1980

"I've spent the last 3 winters in Hawaii and I don't see any reason to stop. For anybody who wants to progress their surfing it's the place to go, it's the mecca of surfing."

"It was then I started living with Rabbit Bartholomew, he'd come over to Hawaii with 100 dollars in his pocket and a lot of high hopes, and had done well enough to survive. That was the year he came 3rd in the Smirnoff. It made me think if he can do it, maybe I can too."

AUSTRALIA, THE STUBBIES, 1981

"I'm afraid I was knocked out in the first round 'cos I drew a hard heat."

TED ZOOMS IN ON SURFERS' MISTAKES, 1982

In Australia Ted becomes a videographer, employed by other surfers, such as Shaun Tomson and Simon Anderson and Richard Cram. "Basically I video tape every heat they are involved in and afterwards we review them to see where they made their mistakes and what they have to do to win the next heat or contest." Ted is going to open up his video service "to any surfer who wants to enhance his competitive abilities."

SUN AND FUN

"For the last 3 years Ted has been head coach at the Sun & Fun School of Surfing based on the Gold Coast of Australia, which has helped surfers of all abilities from beginner to some of the top 10 pro surfers in the world."

There are reports of his marriage, his wife Susan ("petite and softly spoken") and a cat called Sabre (named to honour his father's swordsmanship), and appearances in Japanese soft drink commercials, with a footnote to do with epilepsy: "About 3 years ago he fell from the top of a huge wave, hitting his head on his surfboard." He suffered a concussion and collapsed in an epileptic fit four months later. Doctors warned him never to surf again.

LORD OF THE WAVES
"I'm more concerned with the titles I win myself than those I inherited."

LORD TED PUTS IT TOGETHER FOR CHARITY.
In 1994 he teaches a blind boy to surf at Haleiwa. Says the boy, "It's the best day I've ever had."

And then there are the OBITUARIES. And...

REGRETS
"The only thing I regret is not being committed to surfing a lot earlier in my life."

But I have to mention what was one of Ted's proudest achievements and which was not given the attention it deserved. We are in Hawaii, the winter of 1978. Ted has turned pro, perhaps inspired by that meeting with Prince Charles. And the advice of PJ. He is only twenty-one. He reaches the semifinals of the José Cuervo classic (successor to the Smirnoff), ripping up four-metre waves at Sunset Beach. He is only defeated by

Shaun Tomson, who goes on to win the event. Still, a break-through result. Like an unseeded, unfancied 1000-1 outsider reaching the semis at Wimbledon. Back then there was no Times man on the spot to broadcast word of Ted's exploits. So he took the initiative and phoned up a number of newspapers in England to tell them the glad tidings himself. Forced to blow his own trumpet. But no one would accept reverse charges. One editor had asked to be kept informed, but he was on holiday when Ted called. News of his near-victory sank without trace. He was a hero, but the unsung kind. The best ever result in Hawaii for an English surfer (until then), and no one took a blind bit of notice. His triumph was soured by the bitterness of neglect.

Ted never managed to repeat the result or better it.

17.

His parents divorced when he was only six. Ted never really got over it.

Which explains the following remark in a letter from Hawaii to filmmaker Dick Hoole in Australia, written on January 4, 1980. "I've been busy having both my mom and my dad here for Christmas. It was a real buzz to have a family one for the first time." A blissful, almost Dickens-worthy evocation of Christmas on the North Shore, 1979. I imagine it must have moved Dick. With some reason. Ted was now a fully-fledged pro, renting a house in Haleiwa, with his eye on the imminent challenges of the big-wave season. There was no going back. But at the same time he was going back, and acting as a matchmaker. On behalf of his own parents. With infinite manoeuvring, worthy of Montgomery and his tanks, Ted had managed to persuade both his mother and father to come and join him on the North Shore. He was trying to stick them back together again. To his mind, they belonged together. The only thing was, he had neglected to mention to either one that the ex would be there. He was a go-between, engineering a reunion, only the people he was going between had no idea. It was supposed to be a big surprise. With Ted playing some kind of Eros figure in shorts. Maybe, he fondly supposed, they would renew their vows in Hawaii to the sound of the surf.

This is how Ted saw it playing out. His mother and father would be initially polite, but cool towards one another. They would all go for dinner together at Haleiwa Joe's, driving in Bill's rented Cadillac. There would be a spark of romance over the hors d'oeuvre and the first glass of rioja. Full-on reignited love by the entrée. By coffee and liqueurs they would be flirting madly again like lovebirds. Bill would apologise for all his remarks over the ages about Mimi's suitability as either mother or wife and blame it on the drink. She would forgive him and ask him similarly to delete her remarks regarding him being a misshapen, retarded product of centuries of in-breeding. Bill would burst out laughing and they would be having a second honeymoon, maybe on Maui. The fronds of palm trees wafting amid sultry breezes. A climactic wave crashing on the shore. And all would be well with the world.

So, at least, you might infer reading Ted's letter. A full-on Hollywood production, Hawaiian-style. The sad facts tell a different tale. Not that Ted was lying exactly, more being economical and rose-tinted with the truth. In reality, Mimi arrived in Haleiwa first. She was delighted to be in Hawaii and to see Ted again. But as soon as she got wind that Bill was on his way, she turned around and fled and took the next plane back to the mainland. Ted or no Ted, she couldn't face Bill again. Not after he had had her chucked in jail.

So, contrary to Ted's fond imaginings, Bill and Mimi renewed their divorce decree in Hawaii. Bill stayed on and spent Xmas with Ted and his friend and protégé Tim Barrow. At least they got to drive around in Bill's huge rented Cadillac. That part of the dream came true. Thus, as per the letter, he really had been looking after both parents, but consecutively rather than simultaneously. There was to be no second honeymoon after all. The dream of the real "family" Christmas was over before it ever really began. Except in Ted's warm-hearted reconstruction.

Bill and Mimi didn't even see one another, not this time. They would only be reunited in Hawaii on the occasion of Ted's funeral nearly two decades later, when Mimi would say to the new Countess of Coventry, Bill's fourth wife, "He's *my* son, not your son."

The Hawaiian Christmas reunion was another of Ted's doomed attempts to rectify the world in accordance with a film script. But perhaps if he could have pulled it off and glued them back together then his other mission impossible—to become surfing champion of the world—might not have been out of his reach. He looked to surfing to recompose the figure of harmony that had been lacking in his own life. And—as promised by Captain Cook's surgeon, William Anderson, back in 1769, on witnessing surfing for the first time in Tahiti—to "allay perturbation of mind."

18.

I followed Ted and Captain Cook to Australia. Which is where I came across Dick Hoole.

"I'm dysfunctional," Dick Hoole said.

He didn't seem that dysfunctional to me.

For one thing, even at the age of sixty-something, Dick clambered around the vertiginous rock on which his house was perched like a particularly agile mountain goat in shorts.

And for another thing he always had the big picture in his mind. I went there with an idea of trying to get the small picture straight in my mind, one involving Ted and exactly what went wrong in his life, but Dick preferred to concentrate on the big picture. The wide-angle view rather than the close-up. The view from his lonely crag in Coorabel, in New South Wales, was made for that kind of lens. You could see Byron Bay several miles distant, way down, where the sky meets the sea. There was a lot of space between his place and there, together with cows, sheep, some mad dogs and bats too, if not in Dick's belfry at least flying freely through his living room at certain times. The sound of waves breaking was only rarely going to keep you awake at night.

Dick thought that if not for the animals keeping it at bay, and the occasional chainsaw, the rainforest would soon take over here. And there were a lot of trees roundabout, some of them bearing fruit–avocado, mango, Tahitian lime and mandarin. And macadamia nuts. We had fresh milk from the cows and nuts from the trees. We were poised between self-sufficient and suicide. If you slipped it was a hell of a long way down.

I thought he could have mentioned a few significant details, such as that I really needed a 4x4 even to drive up here. The "driveway" was like an assault course, fraught with peril, and almost impassable to my little rented Hyundai. He said he liked it that way, it tended to deter unwanted visitors. He told me that an Australian pop star was clamoring to move up here to escape her fans for a while. He liked the splendid isolation and tended to scorn the madding crowds down below.

"Turns out surfers are not idiots after all," he said, as we sat on the veranda, surveying the surf from our high point.

"Never thought they were."

"Look at the solar system," he said.

"I'm looking at it," I said.

"Ours is the only blue planet. You'd better get out there and enjoy it while it's still around." He was conscious that there was only a finite amount of water in the solar system and we were using up a lot of it.

"I don't know how long the universe has been around," he said, contemplatively. "Or how big it is exactly." He was always contemplative and he had these blue eyes that seemed to see a long long way, like some kind of telescope or X-ray device. I was surprised he didn't know, to be honest. I think he had a pretty good idea. "But I don't think God made it in seven days flat."

"It was only six," I said. "One day of rest."

"Either way. Let's say the Earth is around five or six billion years old. It wasn't that much fun for a long while. Took a lot of trees to make all the oxygen we need to keep breathing. And surfers have been the great explorers. They are the Vasco da Gamas of our day. They're the thin end of the wedge. Always pushing further—whether it's out here, to Byron, or Indo–G-Land, Cloud 9. Strictly for selfish reasons, but they do it. And they've changed the world. For good or ill." He thought it was mostly good. Which would include Ted.

Dick's first film was "Tubular Swells" (1975, made with Jack McCoy). He filmed Ted in "Storm Riders" (1982), a segment in which he is fanatically training every day, pumping hard at the gym, pounding the tarmac, rehearsing mystic tai chi moves, making light of heavy waves, dedicating his entire life to being a pro surfer, and "Asian Paradise" (1984), in which he rides possibly the tube of his life in Padang Padang. "Everyone says," says Ted, "'What are you going to do when you get older?' But I can't be like everyone else." Maybe he didn't want to get any older.

For Dick, Ted was only a small part of the bigger picture. But everyone was small. "Look at us," Dick said. His partner of many years, an Indonesian woman, had died only a year or so before and he was mostly living on his own and he had been storing all this up for a while. "If you consider the billions of stars that litter the universe…" (yes, he used the word "litter," as if they had been tossed out of the passing car of some tearaway young deities) "…then ours is just a speck. It's like a single grain of sand in the Sahara."

"Yeah, true," I said. "But every grain of sand contains infinity," I said.

There was a lot of sand in Byron Bay. And Lennox Head. Which is what had drawn the surfers here back in the sixties. Not so much the sand as the perfect waves breaking off the headlands, peeling slowly, geometrically, forgivingly. The Americans who came here thought it easily surpassed Malibu and the whole of the West Coast. This in fact was the most easterly point, on another continent, in a different hemisphere, and therefore a natural destination for Californians. Also Australians running away from the big cities to the south and north. Byron Bay is somewhere in the middle between Sydney (New South Wales) and Brisbane (Queensland). Whales sail majestically by on their mysterious migratory way north or south, in search of sex (south) or food (north). Maybe it wasn't that mysterious. Sheep were the same, Dick said.

"They only come to me for food though."

Ted wrote to Dick that he was "migrating to Oz." He'd had enough of England. "All the ice melting in Scotland is keeping the water icy when it should be ok by now." His letter concluded: "I just want to enjoy surfing while I'm still young enough." He started off renting Dick's garage. But as he watched Dick building his house in Byron Bay (back at the beginning of the '80s)–he nicknamed it "Hooligan Mansion"– Ted was inspired to build his own kit house, made out of glass and timber, in Burleigh Heads on a bluff overlooking the Gold Coast. When I saw pictures of it I thought he had put it together back to front or inside out. But Ted liked it.

Then again, he thought of selling up the time he discovered funnel web spiders in the spa.

The house couldn't have been too sturdy because it was eventually knocked off its foundation by a drunk driver ploughing into it.

And then Ted met Susan.

19.

But first came Margaret.

She knew all about Lola and had a theory about how Ted had died. She may have been the first person I met to mention the word "murder." But she was the one and only woman I came across who referred to Ted as her "protector," her "saviour," her "knight in shining armour." Ted would have liked that. I think she once used the phrase "guardian angel" (something Ted could have used himself, as it turned out). Margaret Dupré was blonde, she tended to wear minimal clothing, and she turned Ted down. I caught up with her in a hospital in Hollywood where she was being treated for a heart condition, and had various wires attached to her, but still seemed in robust health.

When she conceived the idea of going Downunder, Margaret was a young mother of three, living in darkest Essex, England. A single, entirely solo mother, who–under the influence of an evangelical uncle–had converted to Mormonism. She didn't smoke and she didn't drink. She was aged twenty-seven. And India, her eldest, had asthma. A doctor suggested the Australian climate would suit her better. Margaret was offered a job as a teacher by the benevolent Fairbridge Society and so, in February 1977, they all took flight, Margaret Dupré, India, aged four, and her brother (nine) and sister (three), full of hopes and dreams of a new life in the sun, inspired by black-and-white government films of children having fun and games, snatches of Waltzing Matilda, kangaroos and koalas.

The wonderful Fairbridge Society (or "Society for the Furtherance of Child Emigration to the Colonies") people were there to welcome them all on Australian soil, as per the deal. Almost nothing else, however, was quite as described. The "Vision Splendid" in the words of founder Kingsley Fairbridge was nothing more than a "ruse," a "trick." The job, for example. That went straight out of the window. They just ripped up the contract. Offer rescinded. So much for the Promised Land. They had been told they would have a "cottage" together. In reality the "illegitimate" kids were sent to "farm school" while the mother was packed off on a bus into the city, with India chasing the bus down the street. "Come back!" Australia had a bad habit of splitting up parents and children, aboriginal and white immigrants alike. It was no longer legal simply to ship children from Britain to Australia, as had been the case after the war. Bringing over single parents with their kids was the next best option.

The Fairbridge "Farm school" was a work camp by another name (so much for all those beguiling images of beaches). It was closed in 1981, and the Australian government would eventually apologize for dumping children in orphanages where they were likely to be abused. But back in the seventies, the Dupré kids were, in effect, slaves of the system. They worked up to sixteen hours a day, digging, scrubbing and chopping wood from before dawn till after dusk. You weren't allowed to wear shoes, so you couldn't run away. Trousers with pockets sewn up so no putting of hands in pockets. A shower once every couple of weeks, if you were lucky.

Meanwhile in Perth, unemployment was rampant. There were no jobs going. When Margaret saw a sign on a marquee saying "STRIPPER COMPETITION. $100 FIRST PRIZE," she said to herself, "I can't possibly do this—I'm a Mormon!" On the other hand, she had to get some money together to have a hope of getting her kids back. So she went in. And was promptly rebuffed. "You're not the type," says the main man, in his blunt Australian way.

It was like throwing down a gauntlet. A serious moment of existential crisis and self-reinvention. Just as the playwright Jean Genet in Paris once chose to be a thief and a queer to defy society, so Margaret Dupré in Perth chose to make herself into a stripper. She had been a shy Mormon, who loved art and playing with her kids, still childlike herself. Now she was a brazen stripper. She found some clothes in a second-hand bin, cut them up, and created some kind of Hiawatha look. She put on make-up for the first time and went back to the marquee. She had no idea what she was doing, but she had done ballet as a kid, so she tried out a few pirouettes, ripping off items of clothing as she span. She won the contest, and got a job taking her clothes off every lunchtime for businessmen in Perth. Billed as "The Blonde Bombshell," Margaret took to dressing as Wonder Woman, before undressing again.

She had been placed in a migrant hostel, where she was raped within two days of her arrival by the caretaker. It was a regular habit of his with newbies. So when Margaret snatched the kids—technically, "wards of the state"—and took off with them she was trying to save herself as well as them.

On the strength of having found gainful "employment," she conned the Fairbridge governor into letting the kids out on a weekend "visit." "I told them I was staying in a hotel, so the kids could come and stay. They dropped the kids off. Of course I wasn't really staying there. I didn't have that kind of money. I was just sitting in the lobby. We actually spent the night in a Salvation Army dorm."

They hitchhiked across the vast Nullarbor Plain and kept on going, right across the continent, from West to East. Margaret was wearing red high-heeled shoes, which probably helped. She wrapped the kids in a cloth bearing the message "SOS," scribbled in lipstick. As soon as they crossed the state border they became fugitives, pursued by irate social workers. "Once you're on the run," she said, "there's no turning back–you have to keep going." In many ways, she reminded me of Ted. After a month on the road, they ended up in Surfers Paradise, on the Gold Coast, south of Brisbane, arriving in time for the March 1979 "Stubbies," one of the first international surfing contests of its kind, at the dawn of the professional era. Which is where Ted would ultimately fall for her.

As someone once said, Australia is not a seagoing nation, it is a beach-going nation. Duke Kahanamoku, the Hawaiian Olympic gold-medal-winning swimmer, first took surfing to Australia in the middle of the First World War. It always looked like a better option than dying in the trenches, or Gallipoli, or Vietnam. So Margaret decided to become a legend, an archetypal beach babe bearing an uncanny resemblance to the young Brigitte Bardot. She was quickly adopted as his personal icon by Dick Hoole, who described her as "a free-spirited female who refused to wear clothes." On a poster advertising the Stubbies in Burleigh Heads, she is rated as a "1000-1" outsider. The other outsider, also on 1000-1, is "Ted Deerhurst." Maybe it was the odds they shared in common that threw them together.

Margaret became something of a tourist attraction, beloved of the tabloid press of the era, whether on the Gold Coast or at Bondi Beach. A cover of *Surfer* magazine, dating from December 1982, depicts her as a mermaid being photographed by Dick Hoole. In a way it was inevitable that Ted would propose to her. For one thing she was as close as any living woman could come to Heather Thomas, other than Heather Thomas herself. And she was a ballerina too, of sorts, like his mother. An irresistible combination.

It's hard to know how serious the proposal was. It came with a bunch of red roses. I imagine if she had said yes, it might have become deadly serious. But she didn't. Something now, lying in Hollywood, with her heart being carefully regulated, she said she regretted. "I preferred to get married to a string of violent, abusive losers" (the only criterion was that they had to be over six feet tall: "I was completely superficial"). Margaret reckoned that Ted was "heartbroken" and married Susan on the rebound. "He broke his rule by going with a dark-haired girl." Ironically she followed in Ted's footsteps and went to live on the North Shore, where she married yet another nightmare guy. She worked for a while at Femme Nu, where Ted would eventually come across the love of his life. There was a time when Ted would go every day, she said, immediately after school. Margaret, conversely, would take refuge at Ted's house from time to time, on the run from domestic violence. Which is how he became her "knight in shining armor." And then, after '97, he just wasn't there any more. He would save her and she felt bad that she couldn't save him. So she finally ran away from Hawaii to Los Angeles, where she and India have now been re-united.

Margaret, horizontal in her Hollywood hospital, but still managing to write up notes for her memoirs, didn't believe the old "seizure" story and was positive that Ted had been murdered. And she thought she knew who had done it too. Maybe, she considered, if she had married him that time back in Australia then the course of history would have been completely different and she could have saved him.

But then again, maybe not.

20

Contrary to the surfer stereotype, Ted was not a wild party animal. Most nights he would go to bed around 9. Even 8. He had to get plenty of sleep if he was going to be in shape for surfing the next day. Up by 5 or 6 a.m. for yoga and tai chi. All that training (as per *Storm Riders*). He ate a lot of rice and a green apple every day for breakfast. No coffee, no alcohol. Tea, but caffeine-free. And he loved cats.

I got all this from someone who would know. His wife, Susan.

She took a bit of finding. I started the hunt in South Africa, her homeland. No sightings. I sent a letter to a post-box in Australia (she had written a beautiful letter of condolence to Bill when she heard the news about Ted's death saying what a wonderful guy he was). No response. I perused the pages of Facebook. Nada. I wasn't sure if she was still alive. I had pretty much given up on Susan when I went to stay with Dick Hoole's ex at a house on the edge of an ancient volcano in the midst of the Australian rainforest. Which is when Susan called. She was willing to meet me and talk. She just didn't want to be "defined" by the past, she said on the phone. We met at Montezuma's Mexican restaurant, in a suburb of Brisbane, in Queensland, where she introduced me to her daughter, Mia, aged twenty-one. Not Ted's. Mia was studying journalism and Susan had been a teacher but was now meditating and studying Chinese medicine and seeking self-realisation and "the state beyond flux."

She thought Ted had died because he was too much of a hero, but I wanted to know how they got started.

Ted and Susan met in South Africa in 1980. He was twenty-three, she was only seventeen. Richard Cram, fellow ASP veteran who used to stay with Ted in Hawaii, is not alone in thinking that he was rescuing Susan from the turmoil—the civil war over apartheid—in South Africa. "Ted was an escape raft," he said. Nice idea. Perhaps Ted even thought of himself as rescuing her, a damsel in distress. "You're much too nice a girl to leave behind in this awful country," he said. But the more complicated truth is that she didn't think she needed rescuing and perhaps Ted, in rescuing others (whether human or feline) was only trying to rescue himself. The bare fact is that Ted had met her best friend Mandy the year before. He was in the Gunston 500 that took place every year in Durban, in the Bay of Plenty, on the east coast. This was the first pro event in South Africa (sponsored by Gunston Cigarettes), attracting surfers from California, Hawaii, Brazil, France—and Great Britain (in the shape of Ted). It had been dominated by local surfer and future world champion Shaun Tomson, who had won it six times in succession (from 1973 to 1978). Ted admired Shaun Tomson but he also wanted to take his place. A win—or even a decent finish—in the Gunston would cement his position on the tour and improve his finances. The Gunston attracted huge crowds and Mandy was a chance encounter on the beach. She and Ted had spoken a couple of times and she gave him her number and he promised to look her up when he was back in Durban the following year. Like some kind of migratory bird, he had a set itinerary that took him all over the world at regular intervals, following the currents and the seasons. So he duly returned, exactly one year later, to the very same place, and called Mandy.

But by then Mandy had a boyfriend, so she set him up with her best friend "Suzy" instead. A blind date. OK says Ted. Then he gets cold feet. So he is on the phone to Mandy telling her he has changed his mind and doesn't want to go out with one of her stupid friends when Susan knocks on his door and he takes a look out of the window and goes back to Mandy and says, "I've got this, don't worry about it. Bye." Susan was like the answer to Ted's prayers. All the photos of the time prove it, Susan was young and flawless and raven-haired and glowing, with a great smile. She had the physique of a dancer. And she was educated, articulate and had hopes and dreams just like Ted. She was fun-loving too. They were a natural fit for one another, despite the gap in ages. The fact is, they fell in love.

A blind date with a surfer. Susan was at least as doubtful as Ted. She was, after all, still at school, the Durban Girls High School (DGHS). But it was a double date, so she felt safe enough: Mandy's sister, Robin, was coming too, along with (accompanying Ted) Simon Anderson, the Australian inventor of the three-fin thruster. And Susan's dad, the managing director of Pfizer SA, waited for her outside the beachfront café where they had gone for milkshakes. Over the next two weeks, Ted and Susan see each other several times. They have their first kiss. She watches him get trounced in the Gunston. They have consolation sex (after their second date, when they go to see the Bond movie, *For Your Eyes Only,* starring Roger Moore rather than Bill, alas). And then Ted flies out again, as the migratory bird must. They vow to see one another on his return the following year. Both in floods of tears.

Two weeks later, she got a phone call from England. He probably didn't reverse the charges this time. He wanted to know if she would come and live with him in Australia.

Her answer was not a straight yes. Consider: she was only seventeen. She was also not an idiot. She says, "I'm not going to run away and live in another country unless I'm married." He says, "OK, let's get married then." Who proposed to whom? It doesn't really matter, they both felt exactly the same way. If they wanted to live together, they really ought to get married and do the decent thing. She had to finish school first too—so they would have to wait another six months. But they were unofficially engaged. No ring as such, but it was definite. Her school friends were impressed by the whole idea. A little like running off with the circus. Ted was somewhere between the Wild Man and a tiger. But being a Viscount definitely added a certain polish. In South Africa—a former dominion of the British Empire—the title, at least in 1980, still counted for something, a guarantee, surely, of some degree of comfort and security. In Australia, it either meant nothing or was actually a hindrance. When it came to the wedding day, in 1981, Susan received a congratulatory phone call from Mimi, in America, that went something like this:

MIMI: So you are now the Viscountess Deerhurst.
SUSAN: Yes, I suppose I am.
MIMI: Well, that and a dollar will buy you a cup of coffee.

Sound advice. But Susan wasn't too worried, because it was never about the money. Some said she was a "gold digger." Which was ridiculous on two counts: 1. there was no gold; 2. she was no kind of a digger. This was young love, about as perfect and as timeless as pure romance can get. Everything was mutual, everything was reciprocal. Marrying Ted was an adventure. Like riding a wave. You never quite knew how it was going to work out when you set off. You had to have faith. Ted said that Susan was like a transplanted tree whose roots would take time to settle into a different soil. But they didn't have a lot of time. On his wedding night, Ted got drunk and vomited violently in the back garden. Nervous. "Like he knew he was doomed," said Susan.

There was one major problem. Ted, with his acute sense of injustice, kept reiterating his horror of apartheid South Africa. Susan agreed with him. It was horrible. Ted reminded her of what had happened not just to Steve Biko (thrown out of a window "trying to escape") but also, within the realm of the Gunston 500, to Eddie Aikau. Eddie, a respected Hawaiian waterman, big-wave specialist and Waimea Bay lifeguard, had gone there for the 1972 event. He had been denied access on account of the color of his skin (they weren't sure if it was brown or black but either way it wasn't white). The issue got smoothed over (thanks to the intervention of Shaun Tomson's father) and he was able to surf, but he never forgot and never forgave. Ted felt the same way, on Eddie's behalf. "It really is atrocious," he would say, with a small variation in adjectives and specific cases (of which there were many). And Susan still agreed, but, on the other hand, he was putting down her home country. How would he feel if she were to go about denouncing England (for which there was ample reason, let's face it)? "He was right, but it annoyed me that he kept on going on about it." In the end, it felt very much as he was attacking not just a country but the nearest representative of that country, one he happened to be married to.

OK there were two problems. He had a weird phobia about celery. When she served him up celery he was convinced she was trying to kill him.

OK let's call it three problems. But what she did made complete sense. Even Brigitte Bardot had done something similar with a particularly frisky donkey. Ted had a habit of picking up injured cats and bringing them home and nursing them back to health. He did it with a couple of cats. Turned out they were male and female. Soon they had nine cats running about the house. It wasn't that big of a house. You noticed nine cats. Soon there was nothing but cats ruling the roost. So naturally, one fine day, she took "Sabre" the cat to be neutered. It had to be done. They couldn't fit in any more cats, it wasn't possible. Ted was away in Japan at the time. When he came back she calmly explained about the procedure. Sabre looked the same as ever. Almost. You could hardly notice the difference. But Ted did notice. Maybe he overreacted: "You're castrating me!" he bellowed, as if in pain. And added, "This marriage is over!" before storming out of the house. To Susan it was a cat being neutered: to Ted it was an allegory of his entire existence.

Susan did once go to England to meet Ted's family. She had been amused by the butler and the family portraits and all that. But the reality was that Bill and his third wife Valerie were at loggerheads. They had a "his" and "hers" pair of Rolls Royces. Nice. But in a way perhaps this was a bad sign. Couldn't they drive anywhere together? "Their marriage was already on the rocks," Susan said. She thought it was mainly to do with Bill's drinking. "You don't need another one," Valerie would say. "How do you know what I need?" Bill snapped back, pouring another. He liked champagne. The more the merrier, to his way of thinking. Susan said, looking back on that visit to Earls Croome, "It proved for me that money doesn't buy you happiness."

They split up several times, Susan and Ted. Either she left him or he left her. He felt trapped or she did. Then they would have mad make-up sex afterwards and vow never to do anything stupid ever again. Each would promise to the other. No more aggro. Peace and love only.

As regards the sex: no serious issues. They were compatible, even harmonious. Once in a plane. They agreed it was too soon to think about children. They also made a pact that if the opportunity arose they would try a threesome, Ted, Susan and another woman. Just for the hell of it. They were both willing to experiment. But if there ever was another woman, she was never there simultaneously. Susan discovered some long blonde hairs in the house. Not hers, obviously.

"I hadn't yet discovered the power of denying sex," she said.

Pet names: yes: "Swiney" and "Teddles."

Susan was working in the Blue Plate coffee shop in Burleigh Heads. Her boss Kathy was sympathetic and knew it was a "volatile situation." Kathy said that Susan could give her a call any time and she would come and get her. She ended up picking her up a few times.

Teddles & Swiney with Sabre, c. 1980

One time she had taken refuge in a "grotty apartment," sharing moreover with a "creepy guy," and Ted found out where she was and slipped a card under her door. It was a cartoon of Garfield the cat. The speech bubble said: "You're not still angry?" So she went back and Ted promised to be good. The *Daily Mail* once published a picture of Ted on his knees begging his wife to come back to him.

Another time he said, "I feel as if nothing spontaneous is ever going to happen to me ever again. I'm just going to wake up every day next to you and then we'll have another argument."

"What did you argue about?" I wanted to know.

"Everything," Susan said. What to eat, what to wear, what to read. Whether or not to use the word "whom." Split infinitives. Celery. The scope for disagreement was potentially limitless.

That's just the way it was. "It wasn't all horrible," she assured me. "I just didn't know how to be married." Neither did Ted. "It was like we were playing at being husband and wife."

She fast-forwarded to the end. June 3, 1982. It lasted nine months. A year if you take the few months before the wedding into account. When it came to it, they hugged and cried. There were no hard feelings. "When we split it was such a relief." Susan thought back to the two weeks they had had together in Durban. "Maybe if it had been three weeks we would have realised we weren't really suited."

It was a story with a beginning and an end and almost no middle to speak of. "We were both spoilt brats. We just fought like cat and dog most of the time. We didn't know how to get along."

Bill hadn't made it to the wedding, but he made it over to Australia for the divorce. He more or less blamed Ted, his "unreliable son." He paid for Susan to go back to South Africa to see her parents. But it was a return ticket.

Ted said, "If we're both single in five years, we should give it another try."

Susan's parents back in South Africa read about the split in the newspaper before she even mentioned it to them. "SURFING COUPLE WAVE GOODBYE." Maybe she wasn't sure if it was permanent or not.

Ted still had pictures of Susan and their wedding day in his house in Hawaii when he died. Susan had gone on a date with the king of Gunston (and elsewhere), Shaun Tomson. Ted thought that she was in love with Shaun Tomson. She wasn't, but Ted thought she ought to be. He would be if he was her.

Susan didn't run off with Shaun Tomson. Ted did.

21.

While he was married to Susan, and competing in contests in Australia, Ted went to Bali. "Bali is beautiful," he said in an interview, "I reckon it's the best place in the world for anyone who just wants to go surfing." He had a good-humoured blonde woman, name of Vicki, on his arm, but they were just good friends, it was said. Not a couple as such. You can see her in the video, *Asian Paradise*. Susan couldn't go because her South African passport wouldn't let her. Nothing stopped Pit Bull going though. And it was in Bali that Ted met Pit Bull, possibly for the first time. If Lola was Ted's *femme fatale*, then Pit Bull was his "homme fatal" (and if that phrase doesn't exist, it needs to be invented).

They didn't see eye to eye. For one thing, Pit Bull was a few inches shorter. For another his eyes were hidden behind wraparound shades.

Surfing magazines have two favourite questions in their interviews. "What was your best moment?" and "What was your worst moment?" The highs and the lows of surfing. Intense either way. If I'd had the opportunity to bowl these two classic questions at Ted, he might well have replied "Bali" to both. Bali contained both the best and the worst moments. The strange thing is that it was the same moment. It was "unreal," it was flat for a week, it was beautiful, it was terrible, he got ill, he killed a scorpion. But, specifically, there was that one wave, the one that contained everything, to the point of madness and melancholia. And you can see it all right there in *Asian Paradise*, if you look closely enough. But there is a mystery here: why was it that Dan Merkel turned off his camera? After all, he was getting paid–by Dick Hoole–to shoot the film. But, in this particular case, he didn't.

The friction between them had started well before. They were a large crew of people, maybe there was bound to be some kind of aggro. There was the Japanese contingent, a dozen or more. Which, considering they were funding the film, was reasonable. The director/producer was Hideaki Ishii. Surfing was a growth industry in Japan, and the young Japanese surfers were kitted out like advertising hoardings. Everybody was advertising everything. And Ted was part of that. While surfing in Japan, a Japanese company had taken a shine to him. They thought he had a classic surfer look. In Japan, Ted was king: he was the archetype. They didn't care whether or not he was world champion. He just walked into a shop one day, and walked out again half an hour later with a huge smile on his face and a cheque for $10,000 in his pocket. Ted had dreamed of sponsorship and now his dream had come true. He knew that this was the beginning of great things for him. Hence Bali. In Bali, Ted was like an honorary Japanese guy. Filming by Dick Hoole. And Dan Merkel (credits also include Don King and Greg Huglin and Randy Rarick).

Dan Merkel drove a gold Mercedes and wore a two-ounce gold chain around his neck. He was then–and still is–probably the most famous water cameraman in the surfing world. For one thing, he had worked on *Big Wednesday*, the all-time classic surf movie, scripted by John Milius, and shot in 1977 and '78. Merkel's specialty was to get right into the heart of the action. He didn't shoot from the beach, he shot from in the water, using a waterproof housing around his camera. And he used a boogie board, so he would duck and dive just like the surfers themselves. He captured not just the look of surfing but what it felt like to be inside the tube, hearing the roar, speeding down the line, getting smacked on the head by the lip. Every now and then it could go wrong. If you look at a few frames of *Big Wednesday* very carefully, you can see that, in a shot of the biggest most destructive wave in the whole film, there is—in the corner of the screen—the image of a very small boat about to get crushed by a wave and a couple of guys hurling themselves overboard. Merkel was one of those guys. The boat was not such a great idea that day.

And now Merkel was the go-to guy for water shots. Which is why he was in Bali.

Bali was not virgin territory where surfing was concerned, but close to. It was certainly, in those days, relatively uncrowded. Bali had first shot to fame thanks to *Morning of the Earth,* filmed in 1971, Australia's first big-budget surf movie, and one of the most influential of all time. Bali was the Garden of Eden in this film. It felt like they had found paradise. Obviously the fall of man couldn't be far behind. In Byron Bay, I stayed with Rusty Miller, originally from San Diego, who was one of the small crew of surfers who were filmed pioneering Ulu Watu, the beautiful but supremely dangerous break on the southern tip of the island where the huge left-hander breaks into cave-mouths under the shadow of a Buddhist temple high on the cliffs above. No one had ever surfed here before, at that time. Now in the eighties, it was a magnet for visiting Australians ("We ruined it!" lamented Rusty Miller.) Even I had surfed there, or tried to. Which perhaps explains why most of the filming for *Asian Paradise* was done at Padang Padang, still relatively unknown and uncrowded, the next bay down from Ulu Watu. An almost virgin wave. Perfect for Ted and his Japanese crew members.

Indonesia, as the eighties unfolded, gradually revealed itself as a constellation of glittering new breaks. But none, I think, could have thrown up a better wave than Padang Padang on the day that Ted and his crew blew into town to surf it. And the miracle of it was that Ted had the wave of the day, "the backside tube of his life," as Dick Hoole described it. It wasn't like Croyde when he had surfed some good waves and yet Panda had had the better of it. No, Ted had the wave of the day, no question about it. "The best wave of his life" according to Greg Huglin. This was a wave that was as close to perfection as it was ever likely to get. And the light was just right too. So perfect for filming. Because the two things inevitably went together. The idea of "soul surfing," where the surfer would just go off on his own and surf his heart out and then return to civilization and regale the audience with tale of his exploits, was dead in the water. A mere surf bard, town-crier style—as in Hawaii of old—would no longer suffice. Ted was employed by his Japanese company. They wanted good pictures of him surfing and showing off their brand at the same time. It made perfect sense. So Ted had to not just surf well, he had to be seen to surf well.

And on this particularly perfect day at Padang Padang he really was seen, and filmed, by Dick Hoole on the beach. Ted was on it. He was right in position. The light was good for shooting. For some reason, everything fell into place. He had the biggest, most perfectly formed wave of the day coming right at him and everybody else was out of position. He stroked into the path of the beast, leapt to his feet, and flew down the face of the wave, and span back up towards the crest. Which is when the lip jutted right out over his head and came roaring down beyond him, embracing him, engulfing him in the great churning vortex at its core that surfers call the tube. So easy to lose the line and be thrown over. But Ted didn't lose the line. Perhaps he had learned from hours of watching Shaun Tomson how to steer a line through the tube and keep ahead of the curl. Like walking a rope over Niagara.

I don't see how Ted could have surfed any better. I don't see how anyone could have surfed that wave better than Ted. Here he was sponsored by the Japanese and now he was effortlessly dropping into the wave of his life. And he was being filmed. Everything was working out exactly the way it was supposed to. For once, all of those adjectives on the heroic side of the surfing lexicon would apply: *classic, awesome, epic, all-time*. There was Dick on the shore and Dan in the water. Both of them filming. Stick the two together and you would have the best ever footage of a tube ride, starring none other than good old Ted Deerhurst himself, tube-rider extraordinaire.

But take a close look at *Asian Paradise*. Watch what happens at the end of Ted's ride. In order to explain it we need to

The perfect wave

backtrack a little to the scene with the drugs in the hotel. This isn't in the film. But I heard about it from two sources, Dick and Dick's wife, Carmel. It sort of explains why Carmel and Dick agreed to go their separate ways not long after this too.

In this behind-the-scenes scene Dick is on the floor in their hotel room stuffing hashish into a surfboard. He had hollowed out the fins and the stringer and was pressing little bags of resin into the gaps. Later on he would seal it all up. And smuggle the drugs back to Hawaii or Australia. Mostly Hawaii. It was considerably cheaper than the Hawaiian equivalent, so there was a margin to be made on shipping it over, in quantity. A small network of pipelines was being set up, not just Bali. Dick and others were being used as willing mules. It was how they made money.

Pit Bull could therefore be considered some kind of mogul behind the film, off-screen. Even if he was mainly there for "business." He was "investing," making "transactions." Behind his shades he smiled a lot. The kind of smile that chills you at ten paces.

"You have to respect Pit Bull," said Dick.

"Do you?" I said.

The fact is that Ted did not respect Pit Bull. He did have a soft spot for Sally though. Pit Bull was naturally built like a pit bull (a breed of dog he kept several of in Hawaii). And Sally was his girlfriend. And she liked Ted, too. Of course, Ted would never be crazy enough to get involved with Pit Bull's girlfriend (at least, not back then). But that didn't mean he had to like the set-up. Dick and other surfers were recruited as couriers. Ted was invited to join in, but he refused on principle. He was not averse to having an occasional puff himself, in a self-medicating way, but Ted deemed the smuggling of drugs and the supplying of drugs–the whole half-secret, half-visible underworld that made it all happen– unethical. The early years of pro surfing were largely funded by a pervasive drug-running operation. Morocco, Columbia, California, it was a global system which, in effect, was sponsoring "professional" surfing. At a certain point in its evolution, surfing was more of a cover story for drug smuggling than anything else. But Ted didn't want it to be a cover story for something else. Pit Bull smiled a lot, but Ted was suspicious of Pit Bull and kept his distance. It didn't matter to Pit Bull, he was going to do what he had to do regardless of Ted, it was business after all, and he could do it because everybody else rolled along with the whole scheme.

Dan Merkel was annoyed with Ted because he thought he was getting on his high horse about it. Moralising like some Sunday School teacher. Whereas Ted thought he was trying to prevent young people from becoming junkies. Dan thought Ted was trying to tell everyone what they could and could not do. What was wrong with marijuana anyway? From his point of view it was all just part of the counterculture. Nobody was forcing anybody to smoke anything. It was up to them. Someone like Pit Bull was just providing a service. And if he could get away with a little financing, then all credit to him. It required balls and ingenuity, even if he was mostly getting other people to do the hard work for him. He wasn't so much at risk as they were.

Consequently, Ted and Dan had had words. They had agreed to disagree. But with a bad grace. Ted would never back down in an argument and Dan thought that he was being like a typical English lord, treating everyone else like peasants. And anyway he wasn't–so says Merkel even now–a "serious professional" and he, Merkel, would always save his film for the money shot (and of course this was all self-fulfilling, since had he taken the shot then Ted would have been "serious," but since he didn't he wasn't).

And so we return to the perfect day and the perfect wave and Ted exiting, with supreme skill, from the tube. He didn't make a single misstep. This is truly the wave of his entire life. And he knows that Dick is filming from his position on shore. But as he pulls out of the wave, as it loses energy and rolls on to spill its guts on the beach, Ted turns in the direction of Dan Merkel, who is sitting on his boogie board, camera in hand, poised. And you can see, in the film of *Asian Paradise*, that Ted is addressing a question to Merkel, now the wave has passed. Maybe he is nervous even asking the question. Perhaps he fears the answer. "Hey Dan, did you get it? You did, didn't you? Because that was the greatest wave ever. Tell me you got it on film…"

But Dan merely shakes his head. No, he didn't film it. He had the camera switched off. He can see Ted dropping into the wave of his young life and–despite being paid for precisely this job–he declines to film Ted on the wave. Just to punish him for being such a–as Dan thinks of him–"Little Lord Fauntleroy." A spoilt brat and pushy too. A jerk. And not a serious professional. This will teach him.

It's like a kick in the teeth for Ted. You can almost hear him sigh as he sinks down into the water. Almost as if he had been stricken, struck down by Dan Merkel's voluntary failure, his refusal to film. "Uncool of Dan," said Greg Huglin, who was on the beach watching all this unfold. "How crushing that must have been for Ted. He has his best wave ever, and he had the best water photographer right there, and he doesn't take the shot." Greg Huglin didn't have the highest opinion of Ted as a rule, but on this day he did. "He was world-class—*at that time*."

As it turned out, this was not just a high point for Ted, it was probably his highest point, ever. It was also his lowest. He was stoked and disappointed and depressed all at once.

22.

I took the train from LA to Santa Barbara and met Shaun Tomson in a café between the beach and the railway line. I knew he would have an inkling about what happened to Ted. He is, by some distance, the most articulate world champion surfer in the history of the world, and quite possibly one of the handsomest too. He was a George Clooney among surfers. It's not hard to understand why Ted would fall for him.

He won his first pro event at the age of seventeen. Won all those Gunstons. Became world champion in 1977. Radically reformed and enhanced the way people rode the tube. Won more money than anyone else. Picked up a degree in economics even while surfing. Was the numero uno among surfers for the best part of a decade. Created a whole business out of it and a brand ("Instinct Surfwear"). As much as anyone, he created the Tour. He was a businessman but he was an artist too: where David Beckham thought that he could bend the ball, Shaun Tomson thought that he could bend the wave, curve it to his will. "To do that with a ball is minor in comparison."

No wonder Ted wanted to be Shaun Tomson. Or possibly the next Shaun Tomson. A couple of years younger, he became his apprentice and sidekick and videographer and minder. What Shaun Tomson really needed, it turned out, was a bodyguard. Ted would probably have thrown himself in front of a bullet for Shaun, given the chance. He would have loved to die in that way. But he didn't.

Some think that Ted was well off. He wasn't. He was able to conjure up occasional injections of cash, but not on a regular basis. "He was always scrambling for cash," Shaun said. "On the verge of destitute." He picked up odd jobs, sometimes (glamorously) working as a male model (starring in a Coke commercial, for example, even though he wouldn't touch it himself), other times serving up ice cream (less glamorously) and milkshakes at Grundy's, an "entertainment centre" in Burleigh Heads in Australia. And shaping and selling a few boards. Barely enough to keep the wolf from the door. Then Shaun took Ted under his wing and gave him a proper job filming him. He got to take pictures of Shaun Tomson all day long. A dream job for Ted who would watch Shaun Tomson surfing his perfect waves for nothing. The idea was to enable Shaun Tomson to see what he was doing wrong and improve. But he was doing nothing wrong, so he couldn't improve. Ted tried to chip in a few constructively critical comments. His other job at the time was to teach surfing at the "Sun & Fun" surf school. *All levels, from beginner through to professional.* Shaun Tomson wasn't just a pro, he was world champion. Ted became kind of a coach to Shaun Tomson, or maybe more a good luck charm. So long as Ted was watching him, it was like he couldn't lose. Maybe he would never have lost anyway, but he kept Ted on just to be on the safe side. Once, Shaun found Ted cheering for Richard Cram in a contest.

"C'mon Crammy!" yelled Ted.

"You're supposed to be supporting me, not Cram," Tomson scolded him.

Ted turned bright red, as if he had committed some cardinal sin. Red Ted. The reality was he was only supposed to be filming Tomson, but they both acted as if he was some kind of loyal servant, or disciple.

"Mid-80s–towards the end of my career," Tomson said. "And Ted was struggling. He was single-minded. He had the ambition. He just lacked the minimum level of talent required."

Harsh words from Tomson. But he had a soft spot for Ted, just because of his sheer persistence. Ted would never give up, he would keep on going, come what may. Again, Tomson is probably the only world champion surfer who would think in terms of a comparison with a poem by Tennyson. Specifically the one about the Charge of the Light Brigade. "He reminded me a lot of that. *Into the valley of death rode the six hundred.* Ted was just like that. Into the jaws of death, into the mouth of hell rode the six hundred. Flashing their sabres. 'Flash'd all their sabres bare.'" Tomson could remember the actual line. "Note that line," he said. "Ted had the same blindness to reality." He even added an allusion to Homer, in his hyper-literate way. "Ted was on an Odyssean quest–only without the necessary tools." Shaun used the word "deluded" from time to time.

There was a sentence of his–Tomson's not Tennyson's– that really registered with me: "He would go hard even when he had no chance." It was exactly what made him and also undid him. Took him right into the valley of death, the jaws of hell, to do and die. "I felt like shaking him," Tomson said. "To get some reality to impinge." But Tomson never made fun of Ted. Refused to mock him as some did. Always took him seriously. "He had this naivety and innocence. And you could see the sadness too. You could feel it. He desperately wanted to be one of the boys."

Ted died before the dream ever did. Shaun Tomson was almost like a father to him. A symbolic or sublime father, an imaginary father figure (even if only a couple of years older) of the kind that Ted was drawn to, a hero and role model of quasi-godlike powers. To which he always aspired. Tomson, conversely, looked on Ted as a symbolic son, a young whippersnapper that he could protect and encourage. They went out surfing together at Off-the-Wall. But could Tomson protect him? He was shaken when I told him the story of what had happened to Ted. Or what I thought had happened. But then again he had his own personal tragedy, what had happened to his real son. But, quite rightly so it seemed to me, he wasn't hung up about being a failure as a guardian, he was more concerned with the "bad choices" that people make.

Almost nine years after Ted died Mathew Tomson died hanging out with his friends and playing the so-called "choking game," some kind of exercise in auto-asphyxiation that went too far. Shaun and his wife came home and their son was dead, aged fifteen-and-a-half. They now have another son, born a few years later, but they can never forget Mathew. Shaun Tomson gave up business and now dedicates his life to going about the world giving inspirational "Positive Wave" talks to schools, colleges, charities and corporations with two main imperatives (a) by all means go ahead and become a surfer if you will and go flat out, to the max, but (b) try not to die while you're doing it. All of Tomson's experience and wisdom has been bundled together into *The Code* (written with

Patrick Moser), a bestseller. He wrote it for people like his son, and people like Ted, even though it was too late for both of them.

"You can't save anyone, but if you give them the tools, they can save themselves," Tomson said.

It had lines in it like "I will always paddle back out," and "I will honour the sport of kings," and "I will never turn my back on the ocean."

"Could this have saved Ted?" I said.

"It might have helped."

He said that one million people die every year because of "preventable accidents." But before Mathew died, before Ted died, Tomson himself thought he was going to die, in Hawaii. Not wiped out by a monster wave, but rather assassinated by monstrous humanity. I'm not sure that really counted as an accident, preventable or otherwise. When Shaun Tomson surfed the North Shore of Oahu in the 1980s, along with all other foreign surfers, he automatically became part of the so-called "Bustin' Down the Door" era. Ted was part of all that too, or tried to be. And its figurehead and agent provocateur was Rabbit Bartholomew.

23.

Ted had hung up this sign outside his house in Burleigh
Heads:

THE LIONS' LAIR

You may wonder why. But the first thing I want to draw attention to is the positioning of the apostrophe. It's not "LION'S"
lair but *LIONS'*, plural. It had something to do with the
"Bronzed Aussies." Also plural. This is the period when, living in Australia, Ted sounded like an Australian. Mike Baker
maintains that he had already picked up an Australian accent,
or the beginnings of one, back in England, owing to the proximity of Australian lifeguards. Australia, at this point in his
life, was the ideal place for Ted, like a mix of England and
America, but far from both. He fraternised with Australians
and he sounded Australian. He was adopting an Australian
persona, but with a British twist.

Ted had been impressed by the team-building of the
typical local surf lifesaving club in Australia, the way they
trained on the beach and in the water, and went through their
routines, and did exercises on the beach, and brought on the
youngsters (the "nipper" category). But it wasn't until he saw
the "Bronzed Aussies" in action in Hawaii that he realized

that he had hitherto made a fundamental error: he had been trying to do everything on his own. Perhaps surfing didn't have to be a solo sport. Wouldn't it be better if you had a team around you? "Ted always dreamed of the band of brothers," said Shaun Tomson. "He wanted that more than anything—more than acclaim or notoriety."

In Hawaii, he had found them. Or at least a role model for the comrades of the future. But, like every decent team, they were forged in the fire of opposition to some other team. The name of the opposing team in the context of Hawaii was "Da Hui." Their captain was Eddie Rothman, popularly known as "Fast Eddie."

Perhaps there had been a time when Hawaii really was perfect. Not many years after being untimely ripped from Santa Monica, Ted, now eighteen, was finally out of school in England and he hooked up again with Tony Alva on the North Shore. Tony was still surfing then, he hadn't started up his skateboard company yet. They were both on a mission. "I was like Ted," Alva said. "We didn't care what sacrifices we made." In those days they could live cheaply. They shared a room in a shack on Comsat Road, across the Kamehameha highway from Velzyland and Backyards, and lived off rice and fish. "It was still country then. All we were looking for was waves. There was a kind of purity and simplicity and innocence to it. It was like pure dharma." They would be there for the entire winter season, September through to February, recreating the pure feeling they had had when they were kids back in Santa Monica. The sense of this being Shangri-La. The waves were free and there were plenty of them. What the Himalayas are to snow, Hawaii is to waves.

The swells sweep down out of the North, from around the Aleutians, cross thousands of miles of open ocean, with nothing in the way, and then unload all that juice on Hawaii, a constellation of islands poking up out of the Pacific like periscopes. Everywhere gets hit on the north side, Kauai, Maui, Oahu. Technically, the North Shore of Oahu is more like the northwest shore. Only twelve miles or so, stretching from Kaena Point at one end to Turtle Bay at the other and embracing Sunset, Pipeline and Waimea Bay among other legendary breaks. Off-the-Wall and Rocky Point, they are all encompassed within this compressed yet infinite fractal space. From the small town of Haleiwa to the even smaller Kahuku, on the Kamehameha Highway, via Foodland. But it's as if, for an aficionado of great battles, Hastings, Waterloo and El Alamein are all here, cheek by jowl, in the same palm tree-strewn volcanic neighbourhood.

Alva spoke highly of Ted in this period. "He was physically fit. He always had an inclination for bigger waves. He had big shoulders, a bull neck and courage—and he was a very competent swimmer. He had that desire for bigger surf." He repeated, "He had that. He wasn't afraid. He wasn't the greatest surfer ever, but on a good day, he was one of the best." Life was simple, almost perfect. Ted and Alva, among others, were living the dream.

"And then," as Alva puts it, "the Aussies turned up." Around the mid-70s. Which was both good and bad for Ted, as it turned out. In retrospect, it seems like the beginning of the end.

24.

Rabbit maintained that it was all a big mistake. All Wayne Rabbit Bartholomew had ever wanted to do was "build bridges" and "heal wounds" and "mend" one thing or another. Or "surf hard and then have a barbie and a beer." The plain fact of it though was that his one article, "Bustin' Down the Door" probably generated more wrath and ire and all-out aggro than any other article published in a surfing magazine in the history of the world. Rabbit's shot at beach diplomacy did nothing to calm the storm but rather intensified it. Maybe, some maintained, if he had never said anything, then all would have been well. Maybe–in this improbable alternate universe–Australians could have beaten Hawaiians in the water and they would all have swum back to shore and shaken hands and had a barbie and a beer and been the best of mates and lived happily ever after. But it didn't work out like that. Everything Rabbit said was just rubbing salt in the wounds.

Rabbit's hair is now more grey than blond. But he is looking in good shape. When I drove down the coast from Brisbane to meet him in Coolangatta at Café Dbar (where even the benches are in the shape of surfboards–or may actually be old surfboards), looking out over Snapper Rocks, he was wearing dark glasses. Not entirely to minimize the glare of the sun. He was not only a former world champion, but a "global ambassador" for Hurley, and had once been president of the ASP. He was giving free surf clinics to youngsters, too. But he had the look of a wanted man, a fugitive, on the run, still looking over his shoulder even decades later. There is an old joke: "You may be paranoid, but they really are after you." The fact is, Rabbit wasn't the least bit paranoid. From around 1976, they really were after him. And still are. Especially in Hawaii.

So he wasn't too surprised to hear that Ted didn't die surfing at Sunset.

What happened was this. Rabbit—a skinny young Australian surfer, raised in poverty on the Gold Coast, half Australian Huckleberry Finn, half Artful Dodger, intent on climbing up the charts, with a back-up career as juvenile delinquent—felt he had run into a degree of resistance in Hawaii. A certain *froideur*. Whatever happened to aloha, he wanted to know. He didn't notice a lot of brotherly love emanating from the locals. So he went and wrote his article for *Surfer* magazine. They had asked him to do it and he actually sat in the *Surfer* offices in faraway California and wrote it right there. From a safe distance, it must have seemed. The gist of it was this: "The fact is that when you are a young emerging rookie from Australia or South Africa you not only have to come through the backdoor...but you also have to bust that door down before they hear ya knocking." The "bustin'" and the "ya" were there to betoken a rough-hewn vernacular and authenticity. The idea of breaking down a door was purely metaphorical. He was not planning any actual violence, any more than his Australian tennis-playing role models, Laver, Emerson and Newcombe.

His theme was more to do with style: he thought that the new generation of Australians and South Africans were bringing a more aggressive performance technique to bear on Hawaiian waves. They had been initially shocked by the sheer mass and size and volume of Hawaiian-style big waves, but they had adapted and overcome. They (or at least Mark Richards) had, for example, surfed the legendary Smirnoff event of 1974, held in thirty-plus-foot conditions at Waimea Bay. Probably the biggest surf ever for a Hawaiian contest. Now they had conquered that it was just a question of imposing themselves. There was a certain amount of enigmatic, coded phraseology. Obscure talk of "superhuman extensions of the accepted impossible," "individuals who are making accurate evaluations of their own potentials," "positive and negative vibrations," and "Zen masters." But in translation it was saying: what we can do on shortboards on small waves (with the sharper angled "ripping"–Hawaiians did not rip) we can also do on your big waves. We can "shred" your waves just as we shred Australian waves. The attack was directed towards a certain sense of tradition on the North Shore, a laid-back approach to wave-riding, a mentality. It was Moderns against Ancients. The Ancients in this case being the Hawaiians. "Big serious guys surfing big waves," as Rabbit put it. You could see it as an inspirational team-talk, advocacy for a more competitive strategy, more "radical" manoeuvres, more attitude. Rabbit was trying to will the new era of professional surfing into existence. This was the Nouvelle Vague of surfing. None of it was about attacking things like doors and, even less so, actual people. Rabbit was being, as he put it, "respectful." He struck an almost academic, professorial note, with only the merest hint of arrogance and aggro.

But the Hawaiians didn't see it that way. Such are the potential vagaries of the reading experience. It's more about interpretation than intention. And not everyone actually read it anyway. "They only read the headline," Rabbit said. "You could look up every story I ever wrote and there is not one derogatory comment in any of it." But the reading of Rabbit that got around and established itself as the "truth" was that he wanted to mix it. To get stuck in. Treated Hawaii like it was his own personal fiefdom. The accepted phrases were that the newcomers were "charging" (presumably like bulls) or "going hard." To Hawaiians the clear implication was that Rabbit (like others of his tribe) was a brawler, a scrapper, a surf "warrior," and he was trying to face down or intimidate Hawaiians, like some kind of hybrid of Captain Cook and a white Muhammad Ali (Rabbit had posed as Ali in a magazine and looked up to him as a role model, thus acquiring the nickname "Muhammad Bugs"). White men (or "haoles")– explorers, missionaries, sugar barons, developers, the US government–had stolen their country and now they were stealing their waves too. Well, they were ready for that and they would fight back. Rabbit had lit a fuse. A rather short one, as it turned out. "Live your life like a warrior," he had written in another of his rabble-rousing articles, "as if every day were your last." Hawaiians read that more literally than Rabbit had probably intended.

Fights were soon breaking out all over the North Shore, on the beach and in the water. All Australians were targets. Rabbit was beaten up by a crew of "gnarly guys" out at Sunset.

Thirty of them by his own account: pounded and held under water and ordered to swim to the beach. Pete Townend, known as "PT," another Australian, now based in Huntington Beach south of LA (he holds the record for surfing the biggest surfboard ever made) recalled that he was out at Off-the-Wall when Pit Bull paddled straight up to him, wasted no time on "hello" or whatever, and just punched him right in the face. PT fell off his board more out of surprise than anything else. Later, Pit Bull came up to him in Haleiwa and apologised, which was rare for him. "I've punched the wrong fuckin' guy. I fuckin' hate that guy." The right guy was probably Rabbit (or possibly Ian "Kanga" Cairns). It wasn't the roughing up of someone that he was sorry about, it was just he had missed his original target. But this was a time when everyone who was not from Hawaii was a potential target. If you were there, it was just naturally assumed you were looking for trouble. The so-called "impact zone" (where you were liable to get stomped on by a collapsing wave) had taken on a new and more sinister connotation. In fact, the impact zone had expanded and enveloped the island. Rabbit had got into a "tussle" with visiting Hawaiian Barry Kanaiaupuni during a contest in South Africa. In the same period he was caught up in a riot on a beach in California. He was a marked man.

After a number of clashes on the North Shore, Rabbit and his fellow Australians were forced to take refuge in a house on the Kuilima Estate at Turtle Bay (where Ted would eventually go to live, and finally die). For a while Rabbit (with, rumour had it, contracts out on his life) had actually been hiding in the bushes around Kammieland. Except for fleeting appearances in contests, they were in exile. Rabbit was persona non grata. Public Enemy No. 1. Australians slept with baseball bats under their beds (Rabbit said he only had a tennis racquet, because he spent a lot of time learning to play tennis at Turtle Bay, prohibited as he was from the beach). Shaun Tomson, having been roughed up time and again and told to leave the island, went so far as to acquire a shotgun. Purely for self-defence. He slept with it by his bed, within easy reach. You never knew. Hawaii was part tropical paradise, part war zone. Another guy kept a gun in the glove compartment of his car. There was a siege mentality on both sides.

Then the Aikaus stepped in. The Aikau family had the right credentials. They numbered a couple of big-wave surfers among their ranks. They were native Hawaiians. One a lifeguard at Waimea Bay and modern-day hero who loved to play the slack-string guitar (and who would eventually die a hero's death at sea). The Aikau family was widely respected among both Hawaiians and non-Hawaiians. A "ho'oponopono" was duly held at the Turtle Bay Hilton, a popular assembly at which grievances could be aired and justice meted out. It was, in effect, a public trial. And the accused was none other than Rabbit. If you want to call him a scapegoat or human sacrifice, I'm not going to argue with you. The Aikaus were peacemakers but the price of peace was that someone had to pay. The net result was that Rabbit was blamed for everything that had gone wrong on the North Shore. Despite his good intentions, the official verdict was handed down that he had "disrespected" Hawaii and Hawaiians. He was duly banished from the kingdom of Hawaii, except that he was still, in theory, allowed to compete in the Triple Crown contests (probably with a police escort to be on the safe side). There was no possibility of appeal. "Rough justice" would probably be too kind, but this was as close as it ever got to any kind of justice on the North Shore.

Rabbit had to lie low for a few years. Maybe he never stopped lying low. It's what he called "getting the Captain Cook treatment." Cook was killed by Hawaiians on the shores of the Big Island a couple of hundred years before, after incurring the wrath of the locals. Beaten to death, chopped up, ceremonially burned, possibly eaten in part. In a 2005 interview, Rabbit would say that the campaign—the Hawaiian war, Black Shorts vs Rabbit—"cut me in half as a man."

"To this day," he added when I spoke to him in Coolangatta, "I'm still paying for it."

Forgive and forget; let bygones be bygones: I've no idea if that ever works for anybody, but I know it doesn't fly in Hawaii. Rabbit reckoned they had forgiven the Japanese Pearl Harbour (at the other end of the island) but had never forgiven him. On the North Shore it's all about a blood feud that echoes down the generations. A low-level war that is never over, just simmering, and waiting its chance to froth over once again. "It goes deep with me," Rabbit said, "but it's affected the whole of pro surfing."

Shaun Tomson made a film based on Rabbit's article and using the same title, which had now transcended the original short essay it was hung on and morphed into an allegory of progress or evolution whether in surfing or civilisation at large. It is possible that the very idea of being a pro surfer only began to be taken seriously from the mid-70s onwards, thanks to the influx of Australians and South Africans in Hawaii with their more competitive mentality. This was what

Rabbit called "the volcanic birth" of pro surfing. "We created the golden goose," as he put it. It didn't exist before them. "We willed it into existence." Surfing had become more professionalised, there was no argument about that. There were more contests with larger cheques for the winners. Nobody used the derogatory term "beach bum" any more. Surfing was almost respectable. Huge companies like Quiksilver and Billabong and Rip Curl had emerged out of the foam (a *New York Times* article of 2008 speaks of a "$7.48 billion surfing-goods industry": there has been some retrenchment since, hence the subtitle of Phil Jarratt's 2010 history, *Salts and Suits*–"how a bunch of surf bums created a multi-billion dollar industry... and almost lost it"). Surfing magazines expanded, largely funded by advertising. Paul Holmes recalls that *Surfer* magazine was less than 100 pages when he became editor in 1981, but ran to 160 pages when he left nearly ten years later. The IPS (International Professional Surfing) the forerunner of the ASP organization, had been established (by Fred Hemmings and Randy Rarick), roughly on the model of the tennis circuit and the ATP. Now it was possible to have a genuine world champion–which Rabbit himself would become in 1978–and a "world tour."

Still the abiding and inescapable impression (intended or otherwise) was that Hawaiians–having provided a useful if neolithic kickstart–belonged to the past while the future belonged to these trailblazing white guys from other countries. Hawaiians were, in effect, a booster rocket that could now be cast off somewhere in outer space while the true surfers of the great beyond sailed on alone. The baton had been definitively passed on. The Hawaiians were old school, they were passé. There was an interview with Ian Cairns in *Surfer* headlined, "WE'RE NUMBER ONE" in which he argued that "because we seem to be able to push ourselves harder than the Hawaiians do, our surfing as a group, has improved outrageously. Whereas theirs, as a group, has stagnated." It was the next stage in evolution. Inevitable. But maybe the Hawaiians didn't see it like that. Maybe they didn't want to be cast off or passed by or pissed on by the Number Ones.

When Ian Cairns also wrote (another headline, this time in an Australian newspaper), "ALOHA IS DEAD," the Hawaiians sort of agreed. Cairns went to the trouble of faxing the piece over to the North Shore, to make sure he got the message across. And Fred Hemmings then duly put it in front of Pit Bull. Which was inflammatory. (Note that this was not Rabbit saying this–recall that he never made any "derogatory" remarks–but it might as well have been, because it all got linked with him in the great collective unconscious of the North Shore).

The North Shore locals had formed themselves into the "Black Shorts" (also known as "Da Hui"–short for "Hui o he'e nalu" or "wave-sliding club"). They threatened to disrupt all the surfing contests along the length of the North Shore until they were given the job of "Water Patrol" i.e. they were asked to get people out of the water who would get in the way, even though they were the ones who were mainly getting in the way in the first place. It was a classic protection racket, pure extortion. They were providing protection–from themselves. The *New York Times* described it as "militant aquatic traffic control." But it was also a form of revenge against the haoles. Black Shorts vs White Guys. An anti-colonialist or "resistance" movement of sorts (according to Isaiah Walker's *Waves of Resistance*). "They may be the mafia," said one local, "but at least they're *our* mafia." One simple for instance: one day, on account of some phantasmal act of "disrespect," a number of Black Shorts invaded a house belonging to one of the big surf companies, beat up (or "slapped") every white guy they could find in it, then left again: and no complaint was ever made, there was no police intervention whatsoever, no charges of physical assault were ever brought, and no one was brought to book on this account. Imagine what would happen if a gang of thugs broke into Apple or Microsoft and beat the living daylights out of the geeks. The way I heard the story the CEO, or President, who happened to be there, also took a beating, from Pit Bull himself: so it was the equivalent of Steve Jobs or Bill Gates getting a punch in the face. And yet, judicially speaking, none of this ever happened. Put it down to rumour. This was just the North Shore being the North Shore. Omertà was the easiest option all round. It was more like Cartel HQ than California. Peace had broken out, but it was only ever a temporary armistice, a brief pause in the hostilities.

It took a natural criminal genius to see that there could be a perfect fusion between a surf club and a street gang. Territory was everything. Mean streets made of sand. Surf wars were essentially turf wars.

Pit Bull had offered his services to Shaun Tomson when he was shooting *Bustin Down the Door*—as the bad guy. Tomson described him as "crafty and clever and utterly ruthless." For Tomson, surfing was a "substitute religion." In Pit Bull he had found Satan. Pit Bull had been arrested on various charges over the ages (burglary, kidnapping, extortion), but he always got off scot free.

Meanwhile Ted, who was all for progress and the fuller development of professional surfing which would therefore, he hoped, include him in its expanded and benevolent embrace, nailed his colours at this time to the Australian mast. He went around saying things like "G'day, mate" and "beaut." Perhaps unwisely in the circumstances. Maybe he should have been more like Switzerland–or Wales (thinking of the case of PJ). But Ted admired the "Bronzed Aussies" team of Ian Cairns, Pete Townend and Mark Warren (later joined by Cheyne Horan) and their "glam-surf" image and professionalism (if not necessarily their matching velour jumpsuits). He approved of a certain raw tribalism, because at least it implied solidarity and team spirit, which underpinned the theory of Excalibur (you had to be a hero, but only on behalf of others, in opposition to pure evil). Inspired by their example, he came up with the idea of an alternative Northern Hemisphere team, "The British Lions." He was one, of course. There were others, now and then. But it was mainly Ted. Singular, but plural in theory. Hence the "Lions' Lair" in Australia. And the Australian accent.

25.

There was, finally, one more explanation that I heard (from more than one source) for the antipathy of native Hawaiians towards the incoming tide of young white men. There was an undeniable ring of truth to the claim. Which was that certain Hawaiians didn't care about a few t-shirts or labels on shorts, but they did care if these unwanted immigrants were also selling drugs and undercutting their market.

Over the years, the type of substance on offer varied, from marijuana to cocaine, from heroin to crystal meth. Surf culture and drug culture had a habit of coalescing. Mark Boyum founded G-Land in Indonesia as a front for heroin smuggling (it's all in the semi-undercover film, *Sea of Darkness*, which Dick Hoole showed me). Andy Irons, three-time world champion from Kauai, died in 2010 in a hotel in Dallas, in rock-star style, with a bewildering cocktail of drugs in his system, for example. Australian Tom Carroll, former two-time world champ, came clean on his addiction to crystal meth; Michael Peterson succumbed to heroin and paranoid schizophrenia. And so on. At different times in different places, with a few notable exceptions (e.g. Ted), they were all at it.

The fact was that a significant group of North Shore locals did good business out of the manufacture or importation and distribution of illegal drugs. And from their point of view, the outsiders put their business interests in jeopardy. On the one hand, they were potential consumers and buyers. The problem only occurred if they were sellers too. There was a simple rule of economics in play, greater supply entailed a reduction in price, and thus profit. That was the anxiety, whether or not any surfers really were packing drugs into their hollowed-out fins. Or hiding it in board bags. Or rolling it up in their wet-suits. Or sailing it in from Mexico. In those days, smuggling was easy, almost inescapable. I once let a guy I didn't know use my landline phone in Hawaii: on the way out he thanked me, took off his backpack, reached inside and handed me a sizeable "bud." It was the North shore currency.

So if a North Shore guy wanted to eliminate somebody, it had nothing to do with surfing style, or "doors," or culture, or a lack of respect, and everything to do with economics. It was nothing personal, it was strictly business.

Ted got it all wrong. He thought the drug smuggling era in Hawaii was over. "This place used to be cowboy land, a hippy heaven," he said in an interview. "Pro surfers made their money from dealing dope. It wasn't even good business. They'd buy a bag of dope then the guys who had sold it to them would come right over and steal it back again. But all that was a long time ago. That era is gone. In the last ten years civilization has come." What he hadn't realised was that it had morphed from a casual countercultural gesture into a serious business operation, and the types of substances involved had multiplied and diversified, and the degree of potential vio-lence towards competitors or even innocents caught in the crossfire had increased proportionately.

When Rabbit realized that he'd been sold a comforting lie about how Ted had died–the uplifting "Drowned at Sunset" story–and that he had been pleasantly deluded for the last twenty years, he thought it just confirmed the widespread discrepancy between truth and hype where Hawaii was concerned: "Don't lift up the carpet. Enjoy the sweet smell and blue skies and the surf."

Ted and Rabbit had always been close, starting from around 1972. "Incredibly fun years," said Rabbit. They used to surf Off the Wall together. Rabbit's mother was a ballet teacher and maybe this reminded Ted of his own ballerina mother. They both came from broken families. They bunked together in assorted shacks around the North Shore at different times. They travelled to France and Cornwall and Durban together. They had competed against one another and Ted once went up against Rabbit in the semifinals of a major contest, in 1979, in the Bay of Plenty (and lost). Rabbit admired his never-say-die persistence, his sheer mule-headed stubbornness and refusal to give up, in the face of all the evidence. "I know I can make it," was Ted's over-optimistic catchphrase of the period. But Rabbit hadn't seen him in the last few years of his life. Now, further down the line, he felt closer to Ted than ever. "Everything changed in '76–and Ted was part of that."

I was sorry to say goodbye to Rabbit because he seemed such a close tie to Ted, a "bridge" as he would say. Sitting in the Dbar café having a conversation with Rabbit, I could almost (like Duncan Coventry) feel the presence of Ted himself. But there was one line of Rabbit's that stuck with me, because even if Rabbit had been deluded about the death of

Ted he soon grasped the essence of it: "They were telling him to get out of the way. But he mourned the passing of that era, and he clung on to it." And he was still clinging on to it right to the end, as a drowning man will cling to the broken shard of a lifeboat.

26.

I was surfing correspondent to *The Times*. Ted was aged thirty. He competed in each of the three French events. "He surfed his heart out and was trounced in all his heats," I wrote. The question was why: why did he keep on losing? (And, secondly, why would he keep on going even so?) He had now spent ten years on the pro tour and he was still struggling even to get out of the qualifying rounds. It was a mystery.

Ted had an explanation: "I've been hosed by the ASP."

There were conflicting schools of thought on the subject.

I for one thought he was hard done by and deserved to get past first base.

The nickname, "Lord Ted," had become a problem. Ted had, in effect, run away from the British aristocracy, but here it was coming back to haunt him. The ASP had given him an entry ticket, but they weren't letting him into the inner sanctum. They had tagged him as a "novelty act," some said. He added color and distinctiveness at a time when the ASP was steadily building its brand. So he got past security. On the other hand, they hung the Lord Ted label around his neck, thus condemning him at the same time to relatively unsympathetic judging from a notoriously subjective system.

"Lord Ted?" the judges would say to themselves (and I spoke to a few of them, trying to work out what was going on). "He doesn't need a break—he's rich!"

The fact is, he wasn't rich. Also (to state a simple fact) he wasn't a Lord. But facts were not uppermost in anyone's mind at the time. This was the North Shore after all. The ASP was still spinning itself into existence. What it needed was poor boys making good at the top, as if surfing was a magic wand for transforming ghetto kids into jet-setters. Which, to some extent, for a few, it was–Tom Carroll, for example, got the first million-dollar contract from Quiksilver in 1989, the year I met Ted. Pottz not far behind.

Ted hated the nickname because it made him seem like a playboy instead of a serious surfer. "I'm the only guy around here who has to earn his living." He was making ends meet by taking odd jobs–as a waiter, a salesman or a gas pumper. At the age of thirty he was still aiming for a breakthrough. All he needed was to be given a shot. "I've got to make it through the next three or four months or I'm dead."

Derek Hynd, the Australian writer, recalls an event in Japan towards the end of the seventies where Ted was up against a Japanese guy. Ted, on anybody's reckoning, came out way ahead. He was manifestly the winner. They (Derek and friends and supporters of Ted) were already celebrating. At last Ted scores, they thought. Well deserved. Hats off. Later on, Derek comes across Ted quietly sobbing somewhere because the decision went to the Japanese guy anyway. Ted became like a human sacrifice, served up to placate the locals.

Here is a for-instance of Ted in action. Make up your own mind. We were on the North Shore, Oahu, Hawaii. Circa December 1989. Standing outside the ASP trailer on Sunset Beach. Ted was trying to dream up ways of making money, as usual. "I've got to make some dough here. Know anyone who wants a viscountcy?" He laughed but there was more than a hint of anxiety in the background. "They've got to let me have a shot. I'm not asking for preferential treatment, only for what I deserve."

I followed Ted back to Randy Rarick's house. He and Randy were old friends. Or possibly sparring partners. Ted even shaped boards in Randy's shaping room. Randy, like some benevolent Hawaiian god of yore, had once smiled on his early heroic efforts to make it on the tour. But Randy, like many a god, was unpredictable and mercurial. He had more recently turned Ted down for an entry in the Hard Rock Café World Cup. From Randy's point of view, Ted hadn't earned enough points over the year to qualify for a place by right. So Ted had to count on a wild card i.e. the generosity of the organisers. But the fact was that the ASP was favouring young Brazilians and Japanese. If anyone needed a leg up, they did–not getting-longer-in-the-tooth, fugitive British aristos. Ted therefore had the feeling he was being discriminated against, on the grounds of age, nationality and title. Hence the idea that he was getting hosed.

He was trapped in a vicious circle: he didn't have enough points to get into the big events, but because he couldn't get into the big events he couldn't accumulate enough points. He was drawn to Hawaii the way everyone else was, the same way I was: Hawaii was the ultimate test. Perhaps a solution. But for Ted it was also more like some kind of weird Kafkaesque nightmare. He would fly all the way over here and then find that they had shut the door in his face. But he had to persist in Hawaii, if anywhere. Hawaii was where you either made it or you didn't. If you didn't make it in Hawaii you just hadn't made it. Hawaii, in the surfing scheme of things, carried maximum kudos, peer esteem, not to mention points for the world title and money.

So I said to Randy, "Ted's pretty fed up. He feels he's not being given his shot."

"Ted!" he snorted. He happened to be squeezing an orange at the time–making a smoothie. He seemed to be squeezing it with some kind of renewed vigor. "I've given him so many shots and he's always failed. The truth is he just doesn't have what it takes. Don't get me wrong. He's a great guy. But it doesn't come easy to him. He sees the little kids come up and go right past him. I can't believe his perseverance. He's worked and he's worked and it's never got him anywhere."

"What about '78?" I said, thinking of his semifinal result.

"Oh yeah, he did great that year. Beat some really hot surfers. But we're 1989 now. His star has definitely waned . . ." He sketched out a falling arc with his arm and whistled, with an elegiac, descending note.

But the simple fact is that Ted somehow managed, this time around, despite everything stacking up against him, to sneak into the Pipeline Masters event–as an "alternate." A couple of other guys had dropped out with injuries so he was in. Over the Tannoy we heard the magical words, "Ted Deerhurst pick up your competition vest from the beach marshal."

Ted scrambled to his feet. Almost ran off. Stopped, turned, picked up the board he had nearly forgotten–a 7' 3" Excalibur. Wouldn't get too far without it.

"Any last words?" I said.

"Right now I don't want to talk," he said, hoarsely, "I just want to surf."

He marched away into the competitors zone, the glint of battle in his eye, brandishing his Excalibur. I bumped into Kristin and Sabine (a couple of visitors from the mainland) on the beach. Kristin leapt up for a better view of the action. "The Excalibur guy is in this? I don't believe it!'

Funny that he should call one of his cats "Ethelred," as in Ethelred the Unready. Ted was not unready. He could hardly be readier. He had in fact been preparing for this all year–practicing his backhand specifically for Pipeline. Barton Lynch, a former winner sitting on the beach, was a goofy-footer, so he surfed Pipe on his forehand. Ted was a natural, so in an ideal world he needed a Backdoor wave (going right rather than left), otherwise he was always looking over his shoulder at the wave (not impossible but trickier). Some said the Backdoor waves were even faster and shallower (i.e. even more dangerous) than classic Pipe. I couldn't say. Pipe looked as if it couldn't get faster or shallower to me.

I checked with a friendly Australian photographer. The sun was just going down and the shots weren't going to come out. There would be no record of Ted's heroic effort. But he was easy enough to spot, kitted out in a fluorescent green competition vest. A six-man heat. A set rolled in, fearsomely rearing up and twisting over and teetering and toppling and foaming and thundering towards shore. A couple of surfers rode away on waves Ted didn't even move for. Then a wave came through earmarked for Ted and Ted alone. He stroked firmly, glanced quickly over his shoulder, stroked some more, made a clean take-off, and came skidding down the face. He manoeuvred smoothly right into the core of the wave, but then somersaulted as his board stalled on a sandbank, an area known locally as the "Bermuda triangle." As the heat continued, Ted was stuck with left-handers (the classic Pipeline configuration)–no more congenial Backdoor waves for him. His next two waves were closeouts. On the first he straightened out to stay ahead of the whitewater; on the second he bailed as the roof caved in on him.

A mile out to sea you could see Outside Pipe breaking–the swell was still coming up.

A siren signaled the end of the twenty-minute heat. You're scored on four waves–Ted only had three. But most of the other surfers had fewer and none better than his first. Ted struck a confident note. "One good wave and two closeouts should get me to advance." He only needed to make 3rd to go through. We waited in suspense. Then the names were announced over the Tannoy. He was given 6th.

"I won't ever quit!" he snarled and stormed off.

I caught up with him later that evening at Crazy Joe's Plantation Village. He was playing a lament on the mouth organ. I denounced the judges who gave him only two out of ten for his best wave. Beyond stingy, to my way of thinking, verging on criminal. But Ted was resigned, philosophical. He had already moved on. "It was fair. I should have caught some more waves so they couldn't underscore me. They're used to perceiving old Ted as a loser."

But this was just as true of Ted himself. There was nothing manifestly wrong with his surfing. But he had lost so many times he had forgotten what it was like to win. He had to start thinking of himself as a winner again. He was carrying a new book around him. I managed to sneak a peek at the title. It was: *How to Increase Your Self-Esteem.*

Ted going into battle

27.

It was Richard Cram who told me about Debbie. I was shocked. I guess I still am. I could hardly believe what he told me at the time. But now it seems to fit a pattern of the post-divorce period. Although you'd still have to say, overall, it goes to show how unpredictable and original Ted was.

Debbie is the blonde archetype of the late '80s, successor to Heather Thomas and precursor to Lola. You can see her in photographs taken in America and Hawaii and Australia. She is tanned and long-limbed with big hair. But if Richard's story was true it would go a long way towards explaining his firm views about sublimation. Specifically, that line of his, that he had "tried it and it didn't work." He tested it to the point of destruction.

I went to meet Richard Cram at the Sydney Museum just up from the Opera House and opposite the old Court House. He was a Bondi guy in origin. He still looked like a surfer, tanned and fit and relaxed, his hair still blond, still curly, with just a dash of grey. He had brought with him an idyllic photograph, A4-sized, that he had rolled up in his pocket. Ted (wide lapels, fat tie, incipient moustache,) had been best man at his wedding on a cliffside in Hawaii in 1983. He and "Crammie" had been good friends for several years. With a swashbuckling forehand cutback (just the kind of acutely angled manoeuver judges were looking for), Cram was a contender among Ted's generation of pro surfers and had once come as high as 10th in the world in 1984, and in the same year had a starring role in *The Performers*, while Ted was still struggling to get through the qualifying rounds. Drawn together by their mutual sponsor, Lightning Bolt, they met in Hawaii and Cram stayed at Ted's place and Ted was still working on the theory that if he hung around with enough top surfers then it would rub off on him and he would ultimately be accepted into the ranks and dine at the High Table. For three or four seasons Richard would go back to Ted's place and they would spend a couple of months together. First Ted got married, then he got unmarried, then Richard got married, and so they went on.

But there were two things above all, in retrospect, that stood out for Cram as we sat outside that museum in Sydney. They were lodged in his memory by virtue of a degree of shuddering horror that they had once aroused in him. And still did. Dark secrets, in effect, that Cram was reluctant to reveal but felt bound to let me know about.

1. Ted wasn't 100% consumed by surfing. "There were times," Cram recalls, "when there was a decent swell on and Ted was more taken up with playing his war games. He didn't really want to go to surfing."

Waves and yet you weren't on them? It seemed to Cram like treason. I thought there had to be an explanation. Ted had not given up on surfing. But he had tried pure surfing and working hard to improve his skills. And yet failed to make a dent in his standing. He had come to the conclusion that it was all about the mindset. Surfing was fundamentally a state of mind. Surfing was never just surfing, it was always something else at the same time. It contained a narrative. And he became convinced that war was the answer. He relived and replayed key battles, mainly of the Second World War. Of course, his grandfather had died in the early stages of the war and his father had been too young to participate, while Ted himself had never been a member of the armed forces. But, on the other hand, did not the whole Coventry tradition tend towards heroism on the battlefield?

Ted identified with Churchill for one. There was no direct relationship, but he often said, "Churchill and I have a lot in common." *Churchill and I.* Not a phrase you hear that often. "We both had American mothers, and he faced initial reverses too..." While, of course, ultimately achieving victory. One winter I came across him reading a volume of Churchill's memoirs of the Second World War. Ted was one of the few readers who felt he was still living it out. "It's only the condensed version," he apologized. "Not the proper six-volume job." He didn't have room for all six in his board bag. And, similarly, he conjured up the ghost of Field Marshal Montgomery, who won the Battle of El Alamein against the forces of the German Panzer division. He simply out-manoeuvered and out-generaled the Nazis. This, Ted thought, was what he had to do as well. Even if the Nazis had long ago been defeated.

Ted, although technically a child of the '60s, often sounded as though he had survived the Blitz, brought up on a steady diet of Douglas Bader and blood, sweat and tears. The first music he could remember was the theme tune to The Dam Busters. So with all this in mind he carried around with him a set of toy soldiers, together with miniature tanks and other instruments of war (I can remember some tiny planes, for example—Spitfires or Lancasters or Messerschmidts, depending). He would set them up on the beach, on a blanket, and replay the battles. One time I came across him masterminding the Battle of the Bulge (which, I admit to my shame, was the last thing on my mind in Hawaii). "Look!" he said. "The way I see it, with a little more armour the Germans could really be kicking ass."

He was also re-running Operation Sea Lion, the German invasion of South-East England. "With better air support they could have got across. Of course we'd have pushed them right out again. It didn't matter what our defenses were like. It was a question of attitude." Ted thought we'd have made short work of the Hun. "Churchill knew a thing or two about the British. He said that when everything was easy we were hopeless. But when we had our backs to the wall…"

For Ted, nothing was inevitable, everything remained possible, it was all to play for, in 1989 as much as in 1939.

2. Debbie.

In a way "2" is a reflection of "1," since again Ted failed to live up (or down) to the stereotype of the surfer. Clearly if you're going to be a hedonist, you have to go all the way. There is little point in the pursuit of pleasure unless you actually get to experience a decent amount of it in the end. You have to do more than just pursue. Debbie was a case in point. Ted had met her in Florida, Cram said. On the beach. They fell into conversation. Ted charmed her. She charmed Ted. They had dinner together. She introduced Ted to her friends. He was almost a trophy boyfriend. No, delete "almost," that is exactly what he was. She could show him off and talk about him being a playboy "Lord" and all that. Conversely, she was a trophy girlfriend for Ted–bleach-blonde and full-bodied. She was as tall as Ted too, and she had worked at a number of different jobs but none of them had really stuck and here she was on the beach, in a bikini, in between things, just enjoying life. What could be more harmonious?

They ended up travelling the world together for a year or two. They were sighted in England too, in Newquay. Wherever Ted went, she went. I don't know if she ever went to Earls Croome. Maybe. She might have met Bill. And the butler. The records are unclear on this point. But there is one thing Cram is clear about, even though, in truth, his view is unverifiable. Because it would be all about proving a negative. This is the Cram revelation: nothing happened. According to Cram, Debbie and Ted were an item for the best part of a couple of years and yet the relationship remained stubbornly unconsummated, "in any shape or form. It was common knowledge," Cram reckoned. Had Ted gone off sex or taken vows or what?

"She was messing with his head," he said. "Kept him dangling. It was painful to watch." Debbie was a kind of antithesis to Susan. Unlike Susan, she did not marry Ted, she did not sleep with him, she did not love him (although rumour had it she was perfectly willing and available where other guys were concerned: she was not against sex per se, only sex with Ted). She liked him enough to want to continue to hang out with him, but she calculated that as soon as she went to bed with Ted, it would be over. I'm not saying she was right, only that this was her opinion. The question is, how long was Ted prepared to put up with the door being slammed in his face every night? And the answer is: a surprisingly long time. I recalled something Ted had said to me: "I've been living like a monk for so long."

It is one thing just lying low and not having a girlfriend and therefore not having sex, and quite another (so it seems to me) having a girlfriend and still never getting into a steamy embrace that ends in naked frenzy. This is surely more heroic or at least more persistent. A lesser man would have dumped her long before. Sex, Ted seemed to be saying in contrast, is inherently absurd, I do not seek children, therefore I am prepared to postpone mere pleasure while I dedicate myself to other more worthwhile, perhaps ultimately spiritual, causes.

At the same time, he was still a surfer and he needed a fig leaf, an alibi. "He had a picture in his head," Cram said. "An ideal." Hence Debbie. She looked the part. It was just that–assuming Cram was right–she didn't deliver. Ted, the meta-physical Ted, was almost oblivious. "He was always chasing the picture."

He would ultimately find the picture in a nightclub in Honolulu. Her name was Lola.

28

While Richard Cram was disappointed that Ted didn't always want to go surfing and would sometimes prefer to play war games, Greg Huglin–on the contrary–was irritated by his dedication to the cause. Which he considered selfish. And he had good reason for thinking that.

I liked Greg Huglin–a man who swam a mile before breakfast and gave up his time to teach filmmaking for free at a film academy, tall, affable, well-preserved and married to Andrea, an English woman with a PhD–but Greg didn't really like Ted. And this is why. I could see why he could still feel– some thirty years down the line–a little bitter regarding Ted. I mean, he was sorry he was dead and all, but he felt fundamentally that Ted had behaved badly. I had to go and see him at his place right on the water, a short Jet Ski ride to the break at Noosa Heads to find out more. Greg was that paradox, a photographer and filmmaker who despised self-promotion. He moved away from California to get away from all the "dickheads spewing all over you with their accomplishments." And he tested out "fifty-six countries" before settling here, on the "Sunshine Coast" north of Brisbane, Queensland.

Greg said that it was still the "Bustin' Down the Door" era when this thing with Ted happened, at the end of the seventies. "The Hawaiians hunt in packs," said Greg, "so naturally the Australians had to team up." Ted had morphed into a kind of honorary Australian, an adopted son. It was still, to Greg's way of thinking, Bronzed Aussies vs Black Shorts. He was once thinking of buying a place near Gerry Lopez's house at Pipeline. But when he went to check it out he found that Pit Bull and his guys just walked in there like they owned it and sat around for a while, smoking weed. "It kinda put me off buying it," said Greg. "On the North Shore it's hard to avoid anyone who doesn't like you for very long." He had a point.

Greg had got to know Ted through Dick, first in South Africa, then Australia. And he had bumped into Ted a few times in Hawaii in the late seventies. He remembered him reading a lot of how-to-succeed manuals. And a book called *Be Here Now,* by Ram Dass (which sounded a lot like *The Power of Now*). "He had the book, he knew all about the theory, but he didn't have that–the ability to "be here now." He was a dreamer." Greg thought of Ted as "demanding," possibly even "desperate," with more desire than talent, a guy on the periphery who wanted to be at the centre. Thought he had "plateau'd out" after *Asian Paradise* and his greatest ever wave that Dan Merkel didn't even shoot (a dereliction of duty Greg considered brought the profession into disrepute). He was sure that even if Ted had made world champion he would still have felt just the same way, obscurely dissatisfied with the natural order and his place within it–at odds with the universe. Seek and ye shall find. But what if you don't find? What then?

The thing that Greg remembered most about Ted and the main reason I had gone to Noosa to meet him was the day he let them down–"them" being Greg and his French-Tahitian girlfriend, Mareva. Ted and Greg and Mareva were at this time all living at one end of the North Shore, up at Turtle Bay. They were near neighbours. And one fine day Ted kindly offered to give them a lift into Haleiwa, which was at the other end of the North Shore, some twelve miles distant. Greg and Mareva were going shopping and Foodland didn't exist at that point and the only supermarket was way off in Haleiwa. Ted offers to chauffeur. And says he'll bring them back again too. He has some old wreck of a car–for the purpose of surf checks up and down the North Shore–but it worked. So they drive to Haleiwa together, at this point still the best of friends. Greg and Mareva do their shopping while Ted hangs out at the Coffee Gallery. An hour later they meet up again–which is when Ted utters the fateful words, "I just gotta check out the surf."

He was talking about Ali'i beach in Haleiwa, beyond the harbour, which is capable of throwing up some of the most perfect smaller waves (with occasional big ones thrown in for good measure) I've ever come across. "Just hold on here, will you?" And they did hold on. And kept on holding. With all their freezer goods gradually defrosting in the sun. And then melting. Until they finally had to give up and hitch a lift back, with half the shopping already ruined. Ted had forgotten all about them. Or dumped them. Either way they had been sacrificed on the unforgiving altar of the wave. I imagine that Ted would have felt bad about it later. And yet still, at some point, done the same thing all over again. The wave was both sin and absolution in one.

Mareva was furious with Ted. They both were. Greg never much liked him after that. The tragedy was that, in some alternate reality, it could or should have been a beautiful friendship. Greg's father was a general in the American Air Force and, like Bill, Ted's father, had high expectations of his number one son. So they had that in common. "We all want our fathers to love us," Greg said, with a sad look in his eyes that suggested they don't always do what you want them to do.

There was one other thing that Greg mentioned. He said he wasn't surprised that Ted should end up going to Femme Nu. The North Shore at this time was full of young "studly" guys, he said—and almost no available women. Women were in high demand, but there was a scarcity. Femme Nu, in Honolulu, proposed to satisfy the demand.

29

There were clearly defined periods in Ted's life. Each had a name, a brand. The Lightning Bolt era gave way to Sabre; Sabre gave way to Excalibur. Which gave way to Lola.

In a way, Excalibur had always been there.

Everyone remembers the legend of Excalibur–the magic sword that Merlin places in the stone (or anvil), and which can only be removed by the true King. All the young wannabes, the pretenders, troop up and confidently grasp the hilt but are unable to take possession of the sword, no matter how hard they try. Only young Arthur, quite unexpectedly, but effortlessly, can grasp the sword and make it his own. Thus he is the One, divinely appointed and sole heir to Uther Pendragon. "Whoso pulleth Out this Sword of this Stone and Anvil, is Rightwise King Born of all England" (Thomas Malory). Some say that the sword in the stone and Excalibur are two different swords, some say they are one and the same, but either way, Excalibur is a magic sword. That sword is like a crown, bejewelled and engraved with mystic messages. If you own it, you rule. A weapon of immense power, but also an instrument of peace. Even the scabbard in which the sword rests is itself magical and can heal the wounded. In the end, as Arthur lays dying, and is spirited away down-river on a transcendent barge, he commands one of his attendants to cast the sword into the water, where a mysterious hand–belonging to the Lady in the Lake–rises up to receive it and from whom, one fine day, it is destined to be reclaimed by a descendant of Arthur, who will recreate the Round Table and the wonderful land of Camelot. Recovered from the water. From the hand of the Lady of the Lake. A second coming. On a par with the Holy Grail.

Excalibur. Everyone knows it, no one believes it, except for poets, novelists and Walt Disney.

And Ted.

Ted believed. He had faith. Excalibur was real. And if it wasn't, well, then he would make it real. He would take a myth and insert it into everyday life and thereby transform the world. He would, in a way, become Arthur. Or at least Merlin. Perhaps he was indeed, if Arthur had any substance to him, through the ancient Coventry family, a descendant of Arthur. He surely had a drop of Arthurian blood running through his veins. Maybe every true born Englishman did. In the absence of a handy stone that he could miraculously draw the sword out of, Ted sweet-talked a few good samaritans into funding a real sword, to be forged by the jeweller Mitch Nugent in England. A blade made of steel and a hilt cast in bronze and silver and encrusted with sea creatures set against some tropical backdrop. "A treasure any king would be proud to wield," Ted announced to the world. Engraved with the words, "The Spirit of Surfing," it was to be awarded to the winner of the Excalibur Cup, a charitable surfing competition dreamed up by Ted. "According to legend," he recalled, "Excalibur could not be defeated in battle, as long as the user would only fight for right and justice, a noble concept." Only

Queen Guinevere was missing–but surely, reasoned Ted in his mystic logic, once Excalibur existed then Guinevere could not be far behind. As it once had been, so it must be again: the present moment appeared as only a temporary falling away from perfection, a transient and intermediate state that could not endure.

The idea first came to Ted in Australia, he said, when he was having a game of tennis with Rabbit Bartholomew. Singles. Man-on-man. In a classic lightbulb moment, Ted realised that the very same man-on-man concept could be applied to surfing. Eureka! A very fine idea. So fine, in fact, that it had already been espoused by the ASP. The Excalibur Cup would therefore, in effect, be a rival to the ASP tour, the grand prix circuit. And, to some extent, an antithesis, almost an antagonist. It was Excalibur vs the ASP. Because the ASP was, as its name implies, "professional" and surfers expected or at least hoped that they could earn a living–or at least pay their expenses and keep the wolf from the door–by surfing under its auspices and participating in its contests.

Whereas Excalibur was all about charity.

As Paul Holmes, then editor of *Surfer* magazine (which benevolently extended editorial support and coverage to the Excalibur project), put it, "Ted was going in the opposite direction." As was his wont.

Nobody would win any money, nobody would be paid a penny, all proceeds would go directly to good causes, entirely omitting the shrewd and well-paid middle man. Excalibur was a vision of how the world might be. The ASP was simply an extension of the way the world is. Surfing as myth and legend–or surfing as a form of materialism, a career, in which you could work your way up the greasy pole. Ted tried to belong to both worlds, but his heart was really in Excalibur, the chivalric code. Chivalry was not yet extinct.

"To gain, one has to be willing to give." Such was the founding principle of Excalibur. The idea was to encourage or enable underprivileged or disabled kids to get to the beach and enjoy the "spirit of surfing." A non-profit foundation was formed, its mission "to promote the sport of surfing, teach its participants the chivalrous concept of doing for others, and to raise funds for less fortunate individuals so they may enjoy their lives." At first, Ted's idea took off. He found established surfers willing to give of their time and energy and prowess in a quest for virtue and altruism. It was true Round Table stuff. These were one-day events involving the top eight surfers in the world. They pulled in the crowds and they raised thousands of dollars for youngsters. The inaugural event in 1982 at Burleigh Heads took place amid six-foot barrels and was won by Hawaii's Michael Ho, beating Australian Cheyne Horan in the final. Perhaps the result could even heal the wounds inflicted by the Bustin' Down the Door war and thus usher in everlasting peace. Ted recruited Australians who were towering figures in the sport such as Derek Hynd and Mark Richards to do the live commentary. Not to mention Australian "Playmate of the Year," Lyn Barron.

When Ted moved back to America in 1986 he took the Excalibur Cup with him. The "Excalibur Cup Foundation" was formed, "an independent non-profit corporation." He had a vision of "getting the attention of all America" and raising at least $50,000 for good causes ("Special Populations," "Monmouth County Seals"). Events took place, with reasonable success in Florida (three-foot barrels and offshore winds) and further north in New Jersey. "Much like in the legend of old," Ted wrote when fifteen-year-old Kelly Slater–the future many-times-over world champion–took the title, "the youngest proved the most worthy." They picked up celebrity support from actress and old flame Heather Thomas (by then the star of a TV show, *Fall Guy*) and Jack Sonni, guitarist with Dire Straits, who was a recent convert and enthusiast. Ted even invited the Prince and Princess of Wales (i.e. Charles and Di) to hand over the prize (a very pleasant letter from the Palace in response regretfully declined).

However, putting on surfing contests, as Ted discovered, also requires the cooperation of Nature. After one particularly flat, cold, surf-free day in New Jersey (previously described in Ted's hopeful notes as "a natural amphitheater" and a "consistent beach break" a mere hour and twenty minutes' train ride out of New York), Ted took the whole event off to the West Coast. Ted wrote, in his Excalibur notebook, that "surfing has always had difficulty attracting the attention of the general media in America and it was hoped that by including celebrities more interest could be generated and greater amounts raised for our worthy causes."

To some extent, this theory seemed to be borne out in practice. "Heather Thomas was his Guinevere," said Paul Holmes. *Surfer* chipped in a whole page in Ted's program wishing Excalibur CONGRATULATIONS. Ted wrote, "The long lines of fans waiting for Heather's autograph in the cold weather of N.J's spring proved this [the celebrity theory] true in 1987." Surely on the West Coast this would be truer than ever, what with the proximity of Hollywood and *Baywatch*. Ted had visions of movie hunks and romantic interests deserting the set and taking to the waves in their droves. It would be a win-win. They had more to give and therefore more to gain. It was, to Ted's way of thinking, only logical. But it turned out to be a Faustian pact. Excalibur became dependent on the whim of celebrities. Would they give a thumbs up or down? At the same time, surfing itself was becoming more than ever professional. And, reluctant though Ted was to admit it, something of the elusive "spirit" was being hoovered right out of it. Sponsors were energetically sought, and there was talk of Disney, and Universal Studios, among others, pitching in, but hard cash remained elusive. No Disney but only 'FIJIAN TANNING PRODUCTS" and "Steve's Breakfast and Lunch." At the bottom of the cover of the Excalibur Cup program, 1988, there is a forlorn note: "A Contribution of any amount is appreciated to underwrite the cost of printing."

Fast-forward to Hawaii, 1991. We are sitting on the beach at Pipeline, Ted and I, waiting for his heat. The waves are perfect, in a way, vertical and tubular, but also precarious and terrifying. They rear up like immense steely blue cylinders, almost industrial, rolling off the assembly line of the reef, then smashing down and pulverising anyone unwise enough to get in the way. As Pottz once said, there is enough skin on that reef to stick a couple of humans together. Ted is fully focused, replaying some tank battle from the Second World War. Alamein perhaps. The sand is the desert. He actually has some toy tanks and soldiers scattered around. He is pointing out that if only Rommel and his Africa Corps had done this or possibly that, then he would have broken through

Montgomery's lines and made it all the way through to the Nile, thus decisively affecting the course of the war.

"How did the Excalibur go?" I say.

The last time I had seen him he was brimming with enthusiasm about the new Excalibur contest. He had a vision of the Excalibur as a "worldwide organisation," up there with Coca-Cola or McDonald's, qualifying events at all the major breaks, massive corporate sponsorship, with finals in Malibu. "Chivalry is not dead," he had written. The rise of the ASP (he was, after all, about to paddle out in an ASP sanctioned event at Pipeline, sponsored by Quiksilver) was an issue, but it was not insuperable. Ted had taken the view that if you can't beat them, you join them, you hitch a ride on the back of the ASP. So rather than set himself up as Rommel to the ASP's Montgomery he had wisely compromised and located the next Excalibur Cup in Santa Cruz, California, the day after the ASP contest that was taking place right there, a mile or two away. Ted had even set up an office in Santa Cruz to oversee the whole event.

It was a good plan: all the top surfers–Slater, Pottz and the rest–would fight it out on some classic Santa Cruz waves, they would earn their crust, they would get the accolades from the magazines, and then they would wander a mile or two along the beach and do their good deed, and dedicate a day–only a day! surely they could spare a single day?–to the young ones, poor, underprivileged, some of them disabled, who looked up to and idolised them. The program struck an optimistic note: "SOME OF THE WORLD'S MOST FORTUNATE PROFESSIONALS ARE PROUD TO BE GIVEN THE OPPORTUNITY TO HELP OTHERS." They would be role models to these kids. Inspirational. Sporting heroes who showed that they had a spark of decency and kindness and *caritas*. Now abideth faith, hope, and charity, but the greatest of these is charity.

"The waves were great!" Ted says. "Blue skies and off-shore winds the whole day."

"So the pros turned up then?" I ask, pleasantly surprised. Not skeptical but relieved and reassured about mankind. I had previously dared to express doubts regarding the likelihood of pros exerting themselves for a week at Santa Cruz and then merrily trooping off to volunteer for a day. I would have to take that cynical thought back.

Ted drops a tank down in the middle of a whole bunch of toy soldiers. They are duly annihilated. They cease to exist. "Bastards!" A definite tinge of bitterness.

"How many?" say I.

"Not one," says he. "Lots of local surfers. They were brilliant. But not one of these pampered, narcissistic superstars could be bothered to haul their arses up the beach for the sake of the kids."

I put an arm around his shoulder. Even if he does have a tank in his hand. "Look, man, I guess it was always going to be a big ask to get them to turn up *after* Santa Cruz. Maybe you could try it *before* next time? That could work."

"Next time!" He adds something like "ha!" and kneels down and starts gathering together all the tanks and the soldiers and putting them back in his bag. Then he stops and looks up at me, shielding his eyes from the sun with his hand. "Sometimes I am seriously disappointed by the attitude. What ever happened to the *Spirit of Surfing*?"

"Every man for himself?"

Ted gazes out mournfully at the break. Someone is doing something miraculous: pulling into the tube, disappearing behind the curtain, and then–seconds later–getting spat out at the other end, raising his arms over his head, Hallelujah. The quintessential move. "I used to think surfing was all about giving." He remembers one of his own lines from a pamphlet he had put together about the Excalibur: "The satisfaction of helping others."

"Yeah," I say, sympathetically. "Overcoming the ego. Being at one with the planet, right? Feeling the force."

"And now..." He doesn't actually use the word "taking," but he is clearly thinking it. Perhaps chivalry really is dead after all. Ted, visibly upset. He looks as if he is on the verge of bursting into tears. But then he stiffens his sinews and sticks out his chin and rests one hand on the board he has standing up vertically, neatly, like a soldier at attention, in the sand. Emblazoned with the sword of Excalibur. He is a knight in armour again, only without the armour. "There is a spirit of selfishness abroad," says he. "We have to keep going and fight against it. For the sake of surfing."

Any reasonable person would have quit. Ted refused to quit. He was the exact opposite of a quitter. Or reasonable. The more he got knocked back the more he would persist. The worse it was the better. It was like a last-man stand. It was like he wanted to go out in a blaze of glory, dying in the desert sands. Ted reminded me of Gary Cooper, the Sheriff, in *High Noon*. All the townsfolk had deserted him. And the train was due in any moment. But he didn't care. He had a duty to fulfil. He would face down the bad guys all on his own if he had to. And what if he were to be taken out? Then so be it. The more alone he was, the stronger he felt, the more empowered, a man with a gun in his hand.

The competition klaxon sounded. Ted's heat was on. He dumped his soldiers with me and grabbed his board and ran down the beach and launched himself into the everlasting maelstrom that is Pipeline and paddled out.

In many ways Ted was ahead of his time. Teaching the blind and disabled to surf. Now every serious competition has a cancer program or a pink ribbon. As late as the summer of 1996, only a year or so before he died, Blackie Blacker reported seeing him in New York, living in the attic of someone's house, surrounded by boxes of t-shirts, with a notion of getting a new sword engraved with the names of past winners, and all "fired up" about a new edition of the Excalibur Cup. And hoping to recruit Bruce Springsteen to the cause. "He was his old self," Blackie said.

Undaunted, unbowed, unrelenting.

30.

There is charity, and then there is the polar opposite of charity. Rugged and relentless self-interest.

We were like the points on a triangle, connected even though apart. Not wholly unlike the climactic shootout in *The Good, The Bad and the Ugly*. We were quite often on the same island, but there was only one time (so far as I know) when Ted, Pit Bull and I were all in the same room together for a short while.

It was one Christmas–the Christmas of 1989 to be exact. *Mele kalikimaka*. I had finished giving classes back in Cambridge (I liked to send postcards back home, which had a habit of annoying people). Now, donning my other hat–or rather, shorts–I was supposed to be following the triumphant climax to Martin Potter's assault on the ASP world championship. But I kept getting sidetracked. Partly by people like Ted, and partly by people like Pit Bull. Come to think of it, there weren't too many people like either one of them. Each stood in many ways alone. But there they both were, at the grand Quiksilver Xmas party, on the terrace of a relatively palatial home somewhere along the Kamehameha highway, looking out over the ocean. Winter on the North Shore: sultry breezes, palm trees rustling, the Milky Way raining down light from above.

Ted was telling me how he had, yet again, "been hosed by the ASP." A familiar refrain. We were discussing his chances of making it into the top 100 this year when John Callahan, the photographer, tapped me on the shoulder. "You know how you've been wanting to talk to Pit Bull–well, there he is."

I looked past Ted. I was using Ted as cover. "Who's the ugly bastard next to him?"

"That's Lizard–his lieutenant."

Ted hadn't really finished telling me his story. He was kind of annoyed. And why would I want to talk to a criminal anyway? "You know he is like the godfather of the North Shore, don't you?" He sounded a note of disapproval, both as regards Pit Bull himself and the profession of journalist that required me to take a disproportionate interest in people like Pit Bull.

"So I've heard," I said. "It's all part of the job. I have to run towards the fire." I wasn't entirely lying. I was only surfing correspondent, it was true, but I was fairly sure I could sell someone at the paper on the idea of an article all about the Godfather of the North Shore. And the fact was that Pit Bull had recently been in court in Honolulu, charged with a string of crimes of varying degree of severity, from extorting surf contest promoters to murder. And a smart team of lawyers had unhooked him from every single one of the charges. So here he was, at liberty, breathing the free air, reclaiming his kingdom, on the shores of the Pacific. The irony was that he wasn't even Hawaiian. He was a mainlander, from somewhere in Montana or Wyoming, the victim of a broken family. More Irish/Italian than Hawaiian. He was a cowboy who had ridden into town and gone native. With some dubious claim, nevertheless, to having 1/32nd Hawaiian blood or possibly 1/64th. Ted and I, both classic haoles, had about as much. And just like Ted, Pit Bull was in exile. In their different—almost antithetical—ways they were both rejects and refugees and rebels who had washed up on the North Shore. In search of a new start.

First settled by Polynesians a millennium ago, "discovered" by Captain Cook in the eighteenth century, its population decimated by viruses and venereal disease (hitherto unknown in the islands), Hawaii was finally annexed by the United States at the end of the nineteenth century, after a coup against the royal family mounted by wealthy American planters, descendants of the original Puritan missionaries who had sailed there to rectify the benighted morals of the natives (one theory maintained that they were descendants of the Ten Lost Tribes of Israel who had wandered astray and needed to be set back on the right path). Queen Liliuokalani was locked up, overthrown, humiliated. By the 1930s, indigenous Hawaiians were characterised, at best, as "beach boys," surfing instructors for hire but sexually irrepressible, plying their trade along the beaches of Waikiki, and apt to seduce tourists and lonely Navy wives.

It will be readily understood that Hawaii is not paradise, but rather paradise lost. Probably it always was. But it is in this twilight zone between what it is and what it could be or might have been that Pit Bull can flourish. Pit Bull depends above all on an acute sense of disappointment. Crime is normal in Hawaii. I am giving nothing away when I say that, over many decades, Honolulu has boasted an extensive underworld, several kinds of mafia, yakuza, hit men, bent politicians, drugs, prostitution, gambling, occasional bombings, arson, corruption, kickbacks, cronyism, rampant money laundering and bodies found on the beach or buried in sugar cane fields. Or just never found—sleeping with the fishes. Similar rules apply on the North Shore.

The mini-mafia that now rules the North Shore draws its strength and cohesion not just from drugs and extortion and racketeering and a willingness to inflict violence, but from the sense of a grievance against the white military-agricultural aristocracy that has called the shots in Hawaii for over a century. Which, at a pinch, could be stretched to include Ted. Or even me.

Pit Bull wasn't tall but he was imposing. Napoleonic, you might say. He had a kind of density to him, all muscle, a thick neck and a Zapata-style moustache. His face looked as if it had been knocked around quite a bit, sewn back together again in a rough-hewn way, but he didn't care. He would take your punches and then retaliate, with massive disproportionality. He was surrounded by a bunch of heavy-looking men and fairly devastating women, but there was a moment when he floated free from the crowd to pick up a drink, so I dumped Ted and seized my chance and introduced myself. He looked at me. Didn't say anything. "I thought that the readers of the London *Times* would be interested to know more about your story," I said cheerfully. I was young and naive at the time. I really did believe all this. And I believed that Pit Bull would like them to know his story as well. Turns out I had it wrong.

"Not a good idea," he said, in a low, gravelly voice, with the bare minimum of grammar.

"The court case in the Honolulu newspapers," I went on. "Now it's all over maybe London deserves to find out about it. From your point of view, of course." I was doing my best to be diplomatic. I wanted to tell his story. He, on the other hand, did not want me to tell his story. He wanted people to know that he did not want people to know. Thus a degree of ambivalence where publicity was concerned.

"What you called again?" he said.

After that he drifted off and I went back to talking to Ted and a few other people. "How was the interview?" said Ted.

"Not the greatest," I had to admit.

Later I went to go to my car, which was parked a little way off from the house down a side street. A not very well lit side street. Before I could get to the car a couple of guys came up behind me and one of them said, "Hey brah." I stopped and turned around.

"You Andy?" said Lizard.

It struck me, forcibly, that there was no one else around. No one but me and the two guys who stood in front of me. All the party and Xmas and the holiday atmosphere just evaporated right out into space. Nothing else existed in the whole wide world but me and these two guys, right here, right now.

The other guy didn't say anything. Just stood there. It was dark but they were darker. Broad and muscular like a couple of quarterbacks.

"Pleased to meet you, Lizard," I said. I thought I should use his name. As if we were having tea and cucumber sandwiches or something. I didn't quite stick my hand out.

"Pit Bull says you're thinking of writing a story about him."

"I was thinking about it."

"Pit Bull thinks that would be bad."

"I've gone off the idea already."

"That's good, brah," said Lizard. "You don't want to cross Pit Bull. Nobody crosses Pit Bull."

"That's cool," I said. I didn't fancy my chances against two guys, particularly these two guys, but whenever I get hit by fear and trembling my voice goes deep and croaky so it sounds as if I'm not scared, even though I am. "Look, to be honest it would really only have worked if Pit Bull wanted to tell me his story. If he doesn't then we can just forget about it. It's no big deal."

"OK, brah, you's a smart guy." Kind of polite but also terrifying.

The two of them ambled off into the darkness.

I drove away, trying to keep my speed down. I didn't want to look as if I was panicking. Although obviously I was panicking. I was trying to work out if I had just abandoned all pretence at journalistic integrity. I didn't particularly want to be a "smart guy," not in the way they meant it. On the one hand, it was true, it would only be a decent story if I had the collaboration of Pit Bull himself. On the other hand, I wasn't exactly putting myself in the line of fire, was I? The fact is, it wasn't even Christmas yet and I had a job, which was to bear witness to the climax of the Triple Crown and write about it. Which would require a basic minimum of good health. I had the very clear impression that if I wrote the story about Pit Bull, contrary to very clear instructions, then my chances of remaining on the North Shore, and still being able to walk, were practically nil. It was a compromise of a kind. The ASP compromised: they had to if they wanted to pull off the contests. Everybody compromised on the North Shore, if they wanted a quiet life.

Everybody except Ted, as it turned out. He would have the chance to compromise and, when it came to a choice, he would turn it down. And he would have to pay the price, accordingly.

I have one other abiding memory of Pit Bull, in his prime. I was working on some BBC pilot at the time and we went to interview him in his house looking out over Velzyland. It was very secure. Gated estate. They let us in. And the director and I felt we had walked straight into a Tarantino film. Or possibly Scorsese. But in any case, gangland. Rather affluent gangland, with extra palm trees and sultry breezes. In his house we found Pit Bull, Lizard, assorted cronies and henchmen all in shorts, and a number of extremely attractive women, in bikinis generally, who wouldn't have looked out of place around Hugh Hefner's pool. The women didn't say much, as I recall, but the guys were having a tremendous hoot. They were recalling what a great time they had had in Indonesia, from which they had just returned on one of their regular "business trips." Amidst all the business they had still found time to go surfing. And they had found a perfect little bay with good clean waves, enough for everyone. Everyone in their gang, that is. The locals who were already surfing there had to get out. "We told 'em," said Pit Bull. "We don't want no fucken trouble with you. We respect you. So if you would just go away for a few hours, then when we've done you can have your spot right back again."

Maybe because they appreciated the rich irony of so-called "Water Patrol" guys—for whom the local spot on the North Shore was totally "sacred" and must be protected and pre-served—just charging in and doing to Indonesia what they had falsely accused Rabbit and others of doing in Hawaii. They were all having a good laugh at that. A regular belly-laugh.

31

Sometimes you have to run for it. There's no shame attached. It's not cowardice, sometimes it's the only sensible decision. I've done it a few times. It was the decision Carmel came to, one fine day, in Hawaii. She realised that she had to get out. "Escape to the Country" was her favourite TV show.

She was married to Dick Hoole at the time and they were making yet another film of surfers doing what they do best in the best light on the best waves, right there on the North Shore. Rocky Point, Sunset, big Waimea–they had it all on tap. It was one of those years in the early '80s when Waimea got huge on a regular basis. Ted was there. I remember him saying of Waimea that it was like "jumping off the roof of a three-storey house–and then having the house chase you down the street." Maybe Ted would have been happier dedicating himself, as Mark Foo and Ken Bradshaw, for example, had done, to the pursuit of sheer size. Maybe have a shot at tow-in, go really huge. But he tried to have it both ways and keep competing on the circuit.

But Carmel had had enough. "I am thankful," she said. "I had fun."

When I went to meet her she was living about as far from the North Shore as you could imagine, in a house she and Rex had built together out of recycled materials, in the middle of the Queensland rainforest, on the edge of an ancient volcano, where you woke to the laughter of kookaburras. She got out of Hawaii, before it was too late.

On the North Shore, she was already, even then, some kind of Earth Mother. They were all like her children, including Dick and Ted. Especially Ted though, with his Peter Pan tendency. "I treated him like a child." She and Dick had once visited Ted and Bill at Earls Croome, admiring the tree-lined avenue and the porcelain and the tapestries and the real swords and the linen sheets and the champagne, and they henceforth became like surrogate parents to him. They had once helped him recover after an epileptic fit in his garage at Burleigh Heads. Carmel did the catering for Ted's wedding (mackerel, prawn cocktail, crepes). She knew not to serve celery. She even cut his hair for him from time to time (shoulder-length then). In Hawaii she would darn their clothes and cook all day and then her boys would come in and devour it all (she makes the best avocado sandwiches, I know—she was mothering me quite a bit too). And then they would go and do it all over again.

"I jumped off the merry-go-round," she said. "I've chosen to live more simply." Which, at first, meant running off with a bunch of bikers. That didn't go well. Then she came back to Australia and married her pottery teacher and they had a lot of actual children together, now grown up.

Carmel has lived a couple of hundred previous lives. She could remember a few of them in considerable detail. In one of them Dick is some kind of feudal lord who is availing himself of his droit de seigneur with her. "We've all been everything," she said. And the same was true of Ted.

"I chose to live without fear," she said. What did she mean by that? I wanted to know. "When I started out, I was just a country bumpkin from Lismore. An innocent." Then she met Pit Bull and Sally. First in Indonesia and then back in Hawaii. She saw the people around her get caught up in drug smuggling and dealing. And young up-and-coming surfers getting hooked and then burning out. Acid had been the drug of choice back in Byron Bay, in the '60s, then it morphed into coke and heroin. "Drugs were a big deal then," she said. "Maybe they still are, I don't know. But there was so much violence that went along with them. We were lucky we didn't get beheaded in the seventies."

Ted tried to keep well out of it. "He didn't drink a lot and he didn't take drugs," she said. He objected to the drug smuggling just as she did. It was something that brought them together in Hawaii and Indonesia and Australia. She got to know Susan and she echoed something Susan had said about Ted. "He didn't want to grow up, not really," she said. "I struggle with that part of his character." There was a disjunction between "the inner being and the outer being." Perhaps his soul had not been reincarnated often enough to attain maturity. Carmel had worked as a nurse and had studied reiki (Buddhist alternative medicine) and was a specialist in palliative care. But she was also like some ancient oracle, and often spoke in riddles, so when she said "he had a fight going on" I wasn't sure if she was being allegorical or not. He didn't have a death wish, Carmel thought, "but he was playing with fire—you play with fire you get burned."

Ted thought he was immortal, which he surely was, only not in this life.

32.

1991 was not a great year for Ted. A letter to Dick Hoole in the Coventry archives, dated June of that year, tells us that he has "no good news" at all–nothing but "bad."

Having been "burned" by women over many years he announces that he is "giving up on them" but reassures Dick that he is not going gay but only "celibate."

His clothing company (Sabre) has just folded. He blames it on Reagonomics.

He is slowly recovering from a leg injury picked up skiing in the mountains outside Santa Cruz when he fell some "600 feet." He has moved to be closer to a specialist clinic near Lake Tahoe. He is "bummed" in particular because he was thinking of competing in downhill races, "Masters Division." And he is not sure, at this point, if he will ever be able to surf again. "Pray for me–I'd like to surf and ski again in this lifetime."

He is "disappointed" by the Excalibur Cup. The most recent edition ("4th Annual") took place in Santa Cruz. Sponsored by Excalibur Surfboards (no co-sponsors). There was perfect surf–five foot and offshore. But only twelve surfers turned up to try to win "the sword of success." And "no media" (the "no" is double underlined). "Guess the Bibles of surfing couldn't let their top advertisers be shown up by an underdog." Ted, on the side of "chivalry and humanity," feels he is up against "the increasingly greedy business world of surfing." It is clear that Ted not only sympathises with the disabled youngsters he is trying to help, he fully identifies with them, too. He describes his charity as "my crusade to benefit handicapped kids (including me)."

But, on the upside, Ted has a new vision. "You will laugh when you hear my reasoning." Inspired by his godfather, who was an ambassador to the United Nations, he is planning to rectify the whole world. "I've returned to college and am being very successful academically." He is studying computer programming but with his eye on law school. "After travelling the world ten times in ten years on the pro tour, I feel I have a good perspective on how the world is, or should be i.e. one place, one people. In the New World Order international law is going to be a very important field." He is drawn towards US law because "the founders of this country went out of their way to create an honest and realistic system (not what it is now)." Ted wants "equal rights and opportunities for every person on this earth." And ("even more far-fetched") he wants a way of "holding to account" leaders who are guilty of corruption. His thinking, he says, has "gone beyond surfing and probably off the deep end."

Later that year he goes to Australia, stays in "Hooligan Mansion," but then returns to America because (as per another letter written to Dick in September) he is trying to help Mimi, his mother. She is in bad health, in her late fifties, and has fallen on hard times. Ted is trying to sell everything in Australia (surfboards, van, camera equipment, spray gun) so he can stick together enough money to buy her a mobile trailer on "a low-income lot." He needs to help her in the near future "because the distant future may be too late." He signs off saying, "I really need to do this for my mother and for my own conscience."

33.

It was one of those perfect days at Sunset. Offshore and around eight to ten feet and barrelling. The winter of 1992. The peak was jumping around a little bit, the way it does at Sunset, so you had to be on your toes. Ready and able. As Ted was. Sunset had become virtually his home ground over the years. He knew it better than the back of his hand, because he never expected the back of his hand to rear up out of the Pacific like an ancient sea monster, a freak of nature, gobbling up the innocent and the unprepared. So he was on the alert, smoothly manoeuvring through the dozen or so surfers and lining himself up for the best peaks. He was picking them off with the composure and accuracy of a sniper. He cut a distinctive figure, standing tall, wearing a Union Jack t-shirt, his long, wavy hair flying behind him, glinting in the light of the sun.

I had a good view of Ted, since I was out on the water at the same time. Not, in fact, at Sunset, but Kammieland, the neighbouring break, a little to the south. "Kammieland" was named after Kammie's Market, the ramshackle convenience store across the street. On this particular day, the lefts were pumping, and deposited you virtually on the beach (close to the bushes where Rabbit Bartholomew had once hidden from irate Hawaiians). But the point about Kammieland is that it's a step down in class from Sunset. It breaks closer to shore and it's always a couple of feet smaller. Maybe around five-foot and verging on glassy. Not the usual North Shore maelstrom. Sunset was a jungle, but Kammieland was a neatly tended back garden: orderly, submissive, manageable. Sunset – the wave that Dan Merkel and his crew had to flee in Big Wednesday – was wild, delirious, Dionysian.

I was a regular on the North Shore in winter, but I still tended to shy away from big Sunset, Waimea Bay and definitely Pipeline (scarily shallow with a vicious-looking reef and powerful cross-currents). I kept out of the way of the pros, so far as possible. I wasn't quite ready, I thought. Not worthy. I tended to go for the line of least resistance, the easier paddle-out, the more makeable waves. At Kammieland, I was surfing backside, going left, challenging enough, but not beyond my powers. I could see Ted in the distance, weaving about, pulling into vast tubes, the size of two-storey houses, as empty as outer space. I wasn't exactly getting tubed, but I was having one of my best days on the North Shore, on top of the wave for a change, rather than the other way around. I was riding my favourite 7' 9" Willis Bros "Phazer," my magic board, spraygunned in swirling blue and yellow, rarely known to let me down. On that day Ted's star was definitely in the ascendancy and I had the sense that he was pulling me into his orbit, dragging me along in his wake, benevolently beaming me up into some of my best ever waves. I looked on Ted as my lucky charm, my guardian angel, infusing me with "the spirit of surfing," even if I wasn't riding an Excalibur. My only risk was repeating myself, on wave after wave, riding one in and racing back out again for the next, tapping into an inexhaustible vein of pure energy. Kammieland was like a convenience store in which I had been given a limitless credit card and I could go about stuffing everything into my cart, without fear of failure. I had the break all to myself and the sun shone down on me out of a cloudless blue sky and the reef shimmered and shimmied beneath my feet. It didn't get better than this. Everything was forgiven.

Then Ted paddled over to me.

I was sitting up on my board during a lull, feet dangling in the water. Stoked. Just enjoying the feeling of being alive, floating somewhere between Asia and America. He must have spotted me while cavorting around at Sunset.

"Hey, Andy, what's up, man?" he said.

"Don't you just love the North Shore?"

"You're surfing Kammies."

"Yeah, it's perfect," I said. "For me."

Ted sat back and surveyed, screwing both hands up to one eye in a mock telescope. We were in the middle of a lull, admittedly. "I must be going blind or something," he said.

"You have to be patient. There'll be one along in a minute."

"Come on, I'll find you a real wave."

"Ted, this is real."

"Follow me. I'm going to get you tubed if it's the last thing I do."

He paddled away, heading North, in the direction of Sunset. I followed. Ted was like a snake charmer or a Pied Piper. I couldn't resist the siren call. He was my guardian angel, after all, so what could go wrong? I was feeling blissfully confident, fired up by so many impeccable waves. Now

Ted was hauling me up to the next level. It felt like a promotion, like a new recruit being invited to join the officers' mess.

It wasn't my first time out at Sunset. I was living in "Point House," painted yellow, one of the oldest houses on the North Shore, overlooking Sunset Point. I had gone out there a few times, or drifted over from Backyards, but the fact is I had never surfed it this big before. I liked it at five or six feet. Roughly my size. I could handle six. This was some way beyond that. I was calling it eight-to-ten from a distance, but now I got into the midst, it seemed to me like ten was more of a minimum and the maximum was completely off the scale. It was big and it seemed to be getting bigger. Ted turned and looked over his shoulder to make sure I was still there, then he stuck out a hand and pointed a finger at the misty horizon, and kept on paddling, charging forwards, on his sword-like Excalibur board, like one of the Light Brigade, or some merry medieval jouster lowering his visor and lifting his lance. I kept on going, trying to keep pace with him.

At first I didn't really register the wave. It was like the whole horizon just jumped up to another level. I could see Ted speeding up though, digging in and windmilling his arms. I thought, there's no way we're going to make this. I'm going to have half the Pacific unload on my head. But I kept on following my star, put my head down and stroked. Ted thrust up the face and sailed over the top of the wave. I was a few yards behind him and the wave was folding but I managed to punch through the crest and fly down the rear end of it and into the trough. It was only then that I set eyes on the *ens perfectissimum*.

It was the biggest wave I've ever seen up close. So far beyond ten feet you could call it a hundred and I wouldn't argue with you. It was the infinite in liquid form. A myth that had strayed into reality. And it was coming right at me. I heard Ted laughing, but then his laughter was drowned out by a roaring sound. The kind of roaring sound that is made by a huge, meaty, macking behemoth of a wave shortly before it explodes. You could say it was beautiful, but to me it looked more like an ogre, like something hanging off the side of Notre Dame, but the size of a whole cathedral. From this close you could see the boils and wrinkles on its furious face. It had a lip like the deck of an aircraft carrier.

Ted turned one last time and looked at me and grinned and called out, "Your wave, dude!" We'd been paddling out, aiming for the horizon. Now I had no option but to spin the board around and paddle like a maniac back towards shore. We must have been half a mile out. I was paddling faster than the time I bumped into an octopus. Now I had a real man-eater right on my shoulder and it was going faster than I was. I felt the wave lift me up towards eternity and out of the corner of my eye I could see it feathering at the top, beginning to break. I leapt to my feet and angled right, looking for the unbroken wall. For a moment I thought I had made it. Then something flipped and I could see the curtain arcing out and falling over me. I was in the tube, finally, but I was surfing it upside down. Which was never part of the plan.

Darkness descended and I felt myself being driven down and tumbled around and bounced up and down on the reef. All the air had been sucked out of me. I remember thinking, maybe drowning isn't as bad as they say. If you're going to go, this is as good a way as any. A similar experience surfing in the snow in Scotland many years before flashed through my brain and I thought, at least it's the North Shore, at least you drown warm.

"What went wrong?" said Ted, hauling my head up out of the water with one hand around my rash vest. "You were looking all set. That was the wave of the day, man."

"Yeah," I said, groggily.

We were out in the channel, hundreds of yards closer to shore. I had no idea where my board was. I was hanging on to Ted's board. Ted was sitting on it, unperturbed.

"You'd better get that seen to," he said.

"What?" I said.

"That," he said. He put a hand to my head and took it away again with blood on it. My blood. "Is that your brain I can see?"

I touched my forehead and it felt strangely sticky, like I'd fallen in a vat of honey. I still couldn't feel any pain though.

"You look like a boxer," he said. "Who's just been knocked out."

Ted paddled me back in, clinging to the back of his board. I found my magic board lying on the beach, unscathed. I was still dripping blood. Everyone was looking at me, like I had just come back from the dead. A passing pro surfer whistled and said, "You're going to have an awesome scar, bro. What does the other guy look like?" There was a note of respect in his voice that I had never really heard before, as if I had now been initiated and accepted into the great Hawaiian community. Now I had shed my blood.

Ted drove me to the surgery in Haleiwa and I got myself sewn up. Ted hung around and paid for it. "I feel responsible," he said. "Maybe I should have left you at Kammieland."

"No," I said. I had a tier of stitches jutting out of my head like barbed wire. "It was perfect, it was just the way it had to be."

It was always like that with Ted, it was the best of times, it was the worst of times. Ted put me in the way of harm, but he got me out of it again. Ted was capable of putting himself in the way of harm too, and all he lacked was another Ted–a lifeguard–to ferry him back to shore.

34.

Ted had just come 231st in the world. It was better than I could manage, but not that much. There were still a few guys below him. A hundred or so in fact. So you could call him mid-table, at a stretch.

What really upset him was that another Brit was above him in the rankings. This kid had only surfed in one event–the Hot Tuna at Newquay–but had evidently got through a few rounds because now he was several notches above the name Deerhurst.

"I ask you," Ted said. "Is that justice?" He was wearing a wing collar and a sky blue silk bow tie. The one crazy day in the year when surfers dress up to the nines.

We were having dinner together at the Royal Hawaiian Hotel, the pink palace right on the beach at Waikiki, along with about a couple hundred other people. It was the annual ASP gathering, a banquet, where they made speeches and handed out prizes and gongs and everybody congratulated everybody else and told one another what a great job they were doing and how the ASP was going to take over the planet. Pottz (another Brit, technically) was guest of honour. Ted and I clapped along with everyone else. Of course, it would have been churlish not to.

But the fact is that Ted was not happy. "I've had a terrible Tour," he admitted. "My worst ever." He wanted 1st, not 231st. Two hundred and thirty places different. A lot to make up. "Maybe I can go for Most Improved Surfer of the Year," he said. He would only have to get up to, say, 131st this time next year and the award was in the bag. Ted was seriously working out a plan—his new military strategy—along just these lines when somebody shot him down in flames. Apparently, according to protocol, the Most Improved Surfer could only be drawn from the ranks of the Top 44. "Damn," said Ted.

He needed a new plan.

Which is when it came to him in a blinding flash of inspiration.

Snowboarding.

Surfing on snow. It was obvious, surely.

"Have you ever done any snowboarding before?" Trust me to be the skeptical one.

"Never," Ted said, robustly. "But, really, how hard can it be?"

He could ski and he could surf. Obviously he could snowboard. He could do anything he set his mind to. Maybe he would go back to France, even hook up with his old guru Serge.

There was one more thing he said on the subject that sticks in my mind. Haunts me to this day. "At least you can't drown up a mountain."

Ted was surely right. At the same time it was hard not to think he was missing the point.

I heard that he spent the next six months in traction, in hospital, being slowly stuck back together. Even when they found Ted's body some years later, the medical examiner noted the "uneven scar" on his lower left back where they had had to operate.

Some said that he had broken his neck. I don't know, but it's possible.

What I do know is that the next time I saw Ted he was in a cage, like Harry Houdini, but still walking about, just, in Haleiwa. I invited him for a coffee but he said he found it hard to sit down. He was wearing a contraption that was politely referred to as a "brace," but it was more like some kind of exoskeleton, made of wood and wire. His own personal skeleton, having come apart at the seams, was no longer fully capable of doing the job of keeping him standing upright, or indeed allowing him to sit down at will. The frame extended for several inches outwards beyond his head and shoulders and stretched all the way down to his waist. It made him look like a large cube with legs. He could still stick his arms out too, I believe. But driving inwards, rammed up against head and neck and torso and lower back were a series of steel pins, holding what was left of Ted in place. Not too different to how I imagined Frankenstein's monster, in fact. Bolts sticking out of his head. He couldn't make a crack along the lines of "I'll be forgetting my own head next" because the apparatus looked as if it was designed to prevent him from doing exactly that.

Some said it made him look as if he was being crucified. Or a saint, about to be burned.

I was stunned. "Hey, Ted," I said, hopelessly.

"It's not as bad as it looks," he said, still able to summon up a grin. "Doc says it can come off in a while."

As always, Ted would have to go right on getting back on his horse. He had put on weight, inevitably, but within a few months he would be back to peak fitness, capable of competing again, albeit intermittently.

In 1995, according to the cold, hard, unforgiving statistics of the Coca-Cola/ASP World Tour Media Guide, Ted had tumbled further down the rankings to 580th. At the top of the tree was Kelly Slater, with 8,480 points. Ted had collected a grand total of seventy points for the year. He was the lowest ranked of all the GB surfers (including, for example, Martin Potter and Spencer Hargraves and Russell Winter). His name appears on the very last page.

But by a strange quirk of fate, the name of the great Shaun Tomson, former world champ–who had virtually retired–now appeared below Ted's. They were tied at 580th. Ted was finally up there (or down there) with Shaun. He must have appreciated that.

35.

If anyone would know it must surely be Warshaw. He, if anyone could, must have gotten to the bottom of what really happened to Ted.

Matt Warshaw was the same generation of pro surfer as Ted. Tony Alva reckoned that he and Ted had a lot in common. Like Ted, Warshaw had jogged along on the circuit for a while (attaining a very respectable 43rd in the world), then peeled off and done his own thing. So much his own that he is now a one-man empire. An empire of knowledge. He is, in effect, within his own sphere, as close as it gets to omniscient. He, I assumed, would have all the necessary facts about Ted, backed up by documentation and video clips, at his fingertips, or at least stashed away at the bottom of a drawer somewhere. So I had to go up to Seattle to see him, even if it was twenty years too late. We ended up sitting in a Starbucks, of course.

Ted may have got caught in "the impact zone" a few times, notably in Hawaii, but it took Matt Warshaw to define the term. He was just as clear on "tombstoning" and "getting barrelled," having become the first official Surf Consultant to the Oxford English Dictionary and etymologist, therefore, of "green room" and "swallowtail" and "dawn patrol." At the age of fifty-seven, former editor of *Surfer*, he is the author of not just one "Bible" but two: *The Encyclopedia of Surfing* (2003) and *The History of Surfing* (2010). He knows everything and everyone. What he doesn't know is scarcely worth knowing. "Warshaw–ha!" said one Hawaiian sceptic. "All he does is collect information." True, and you might as well add, "King's College Chapel–ha! it's nothing but stone and glass." Or "The Empire State Building–ha! it's nothing but bricks." Warshaw is the foremost surfing scholar of his generation.

He was brought up in LA. Tony Alva was one of his early heroes. He was one of the first–the first, he maintains– to acquire a Zephyr board, at age eight. It's possible he may have come across Ted in the water. Then he moved up to San Francisco when he went to college (and graduated with a degree in history from Berkeley, which is amazing considering how much time he spent at the beach). Then further north still, to Seattle, when his wife got a job with Amazon. In a way he is now forced to be philosophical, living a hundred miles from the nearest surfable wave. But he would be anyway. It was freezing while I was there. Seattle is not Hawaii. It's the closest big city to the Canadian border. There is a marked lack of palm trees. Every few months Warshaw goes mad and takes off to San Diego or places further south in search of a peak.

He is to waves what a lepidopterist is to butterflies. He recently created a portal to a website that tells (and shows) you everything you ever wanted to know about surfing, and more (www.eos.surf). Which is where Ted finds his memorial. His place in the canon and the archive is assured, thanks to Warshaw. On p. 630 of *Being and Nothingness* (in the Gallimard edition, the chapter on "Doing and Having"), the existentialist philosopher Jean-Paul Sartre hymns "sliding on water." He says the trouble with skiing is that it leaves tracks in the snow. The whole point of surfing (and similar water-based activities) is that it "leaves no trace"–the annihilating wave folds over and automatically erases all signs of your passing. But the metaphysics of pure being no longer holds here or anywhere else. Matt Warshaw is an anti-Sartre: his entire raison d'être is to capture and disseminate the signs of our passage, preserving forever those mythic, miraculous moments in which, all too briefly, we appear to be walking on water.

Ted has earned his page in the Encyclopedia. You can look it up. Together with the video of Ted in action. But I had to point out to Warshaw that he got the bit about the death wrong. Ted did not die of "heart failure" in "a North Shore hotel." Matt said he was sorry about that and promised to fix it. I'm sure he has by now. He hates error and myth. He'll probably have corrected "Excaliber" too. Just a typo. With his vast knowledge of the archives, Warshaw reminded me that *Australian Surfing Life* had once described Ted as having had "a strangely beautiful surfing career." There was something to that, I thought. Equally, journalist Nick Carroll had a point when he said that "Ted could not get through a heat. Even when he was in form, something would go wrong; he'd miss his third wave, snap his leash, lose the shorebreak reform. But somehow, next event, Ted would be back, the British Lion, trying as hard as ever." That couldn't be quite right though, because he did actually get through a heat or two and made it all the way through to the semis of at least one competition in Australia, as Rabbit pointed out. And again to the semis of the José Cuervo at big Sunset. But still, the doomed-to-defeat view wasn't so far off the truth.

"The rebel side is strong in Ted," Warshaw said. "He leaves the British aristocracy behind to go surfing." Ted was a misfit among misfits. He sought a title to replace the one he was born with but he belonged only to that exclusive category of those who do not belong to any category. Warshaw had done exactly what Ted had done, competed as an amateur, then turned pro, not quite made it, but then swerved off in a different direction. Ted had just kept on going, regardless, relentless. "It's a heroic thing," Warshaw said. "It gives you adventures, a reason to travel, like the Holy Grail. You feel as if you're living a movie. Everything makes sense in terms of that." But he thought that "Ted went on way too long with the dream."

By virtue of dying at forty, Ted was spared "the madness of the ageing surfer." Warshaw was not. "How do you keep going? What gets you out of bed in the morning? That's the trap that surfing lays for you. What's the end point? The whole course of action seems great but…" Warshaw grinned and retaliated before I could even pose the question. "I know, I've stuck with it. There's the pride… I've made it my calling. But that 'surfing is a religion' attitude… surfing is not a religion. It's no more religious than hiking. You can't base your life on it."

But Ted did. Warshaw was not a believer. Ted was. Warshaw quoted Shaun Tomson's Instinct slogan, *Surfing is life, the rest is details*. "What a stupid thing to believe," he said. "You're in thrall to advertising." Good point, but I think that Ted would have agreed with Tomson, not Warshaw. He believed in the miraculous power of the surf to redeem and heal.

Seattle taught me one thing: it's not how Ted died that is so mysterious, it's how he lived. Why would he keep on doing what he was doing? Even Warshaw–with all that limitless information, and a houseful of archives–was mystified. He knew everything but he couldn't explain what drew Ted into surfing to begin with. All surfing, said Warshaw, is "an inexplicable and useless urge." The funny thing is that, even without winning anything, as he planned to do, still surfing didn't seem useless to Ted. There was a simplicity to Ted's credo, even naivety. But it meant that Ted really thought of dropping into a tube and then getting shot out at the other end of it, on the back of a column of compressed air, as a form of rebirth. He was, to his way of thinking, a new man, purified of his ancient ancestry.

"He had a lot of wild ideas," said Warshaw. "He had the optimism, even though you know it's deluded." One good wave and it was like you could start all over again–from scratch–and get it right this time.

36

And yet there remained the melancholy.

"He was just a happy-go-lucky kid," said one of the great gurus of the North Shore. No, he wasn't. He was more Hamlet, "That this too too solid flesh would melt, thaw, and resolve itself into a dew." *Be* water, as the Taoist recommends. Good theory, hard to pull off in practice.

"He was stoked!" Yeah, well, some of the time. Half-hedonist, half-anhedonic.

Surfing raises you up but it just as surely casts you down again. There is a manic-depressive cycle built into the very process. Salvation followed by perdition. When we speak of the "curve," we can be sure that, like an inversion of the dolphin's smile, the graph goes down at the end. Every surfer finishes with a wipe-out. But even before Ted's life ended there was a sense of something coming to an end. The imminence of a revelation or a catastrophe.

But it was good while it lasted. Ted was an incarnation of our love affair with the beach. You can blame Captain Cook. He also died on a beach in Hawaii, in 1779, so I guess the Hawaiians blamed him too. They took his name just a little too literally. Cook–and his French counterpart, Louis-Antoine de Bougainville–imported the idea of the beach as a Polynesian paradise with palm trees back in the second half of the eighteenth century and we have been struggling to live up to that fantasy ever since. The death of Cook was like a blood sacrifice to set up a new religion. Ted, growing up in Santa Monica with Tony Alva and Heather Thomas, thought he had seen the light. And in a way he had.

The beach makes a sedate and misty-eyed appearance in Impressionist paintings of Normandy (Monet's "On the Beach at Trouville," for example) and then more erotically in Gauguin's naked Tahiti paintings. Then it takes off again with the twentieth-century renaissance of surfing and hedonism. In anthropology, the myth of the beach took shape in Margaret Mead's *Coming of Age in Samoa* (1929) which depicts sexually permissive beach girls disporting themselves, and it gets injected into the mainstream via the Beach Boys and the music of Brian Wilson in the sixties. According to Mike Baker, Ted was "not an active Beach Boys fan, but he did love California and they embodied that culture" and he wore "a wry smile" whenever he heard their songs.

According to Freud, the beach was the natural habitat of the pleasure principle run riot. It was where the id went on holiday. Or on surfari. And it is still there, en masse, strutting the multitudinous sands from Sunset Beach to Byron Bay, in shorts and t-shirt, with a surfboard under one arm. But pleasure may be the hardest principle of all to stick to. One way or another, pain is inescapable. I think I first began to have doubts about my faith two or three decades ago when I paddled out at Malibu one April or May and got the shock of my life when it turned out to be as cold as Scotland. Saint Tropez, I knew, from personal experience (having gone there aged fifteen with my best friend Griffo in search of Brigitte Bardot) never quite lived up to the utopian hype. But surely a West Coast road trip would not let me down? Even if it was a Cadillac and not a convertible (it was all they had at Rent-a-Car). "If everybody had an ocean," as the Beach Boys once sang, "Across the USA, Then everybody'd be surfin' Like Californ-i-a."

There is a photograph of Jean-Paul Sartre stalking across the sands of a beach somewhere in Latvia back in the '50s. He is wearing all his clothes and an overcoat and is tilted forwards at an angle to the universe. To hell, he appears to be saying, with all this hedonism *merde*. All you can look forward to is sand in your shoes and sunburn. His rival and antagonist Albert Camus, who hailed from the southern Mediterranean, was the great bard of the beach. And he had a better tan. Swimming is the high point in *The Plague*, for example, and he speaks in his *Carnets* of the water washing away all the sins and sorrows of the world, like some kind of baptism. Sartre was, in effect, heaping scorn on all that beachside bewitchment. But even he allowed that surfing–"sliding on water"–was superior to skiing since you can't be tracked in water. Both the upbeat Camus and the downbeat Sartre are part of Ted's experience.

The lyrical side of existentialism has been picked up in Aaron James' *Surfing with Sartre: An Aquatic Inquiry into a Life of Meaning,* in which he sees baggy shorts and a board as a decent and credible post-industrial anti-capitalist alternative to a workaholic life on land. The surfer thus becomes a "new model of civic virtue," replacing the Protestant work ethic with more laid-back, eco-friendlier, recreational exploits. I agree with James that capitalism runs dry where the sand begins. You can't build castles on sand. There are plenty of examples of Californian court cases where beach lovers (around Malibu, for example) have sued landowners for blocking their right of way and won. The beach is probably as near to sunny socialism as you can get in America. The sand is not a commodity but is collectively owned and free and available to all. Perhaps it is this thought that once inspired a retired colonel, one of the Croome trustees, to ask Ted, in his blunt military way, "Are you a Communist?" (Ted said that he wasn't.) But, paddling just a little way out, as Sartre himself asks in the dark pages of *Nausea*, "What is lurking beneath the surface?" When you stop to consider the Bustin' Down the Door era, was it really all fraternity and innocent fun?

Even the Beach Boys don't say that. In fact, especially the Beach Boys. Brian Wilson was a depressive, schizophrenic drug addict. There is a suggestion, in "Wouldn't It Be Nice," of Aaron James-style mystic well-being, but the song effectively postpones all the good vibrations, locating them in some hazy, indeterminate future. Everything you really want is in the conditional tense: *wouldn't it be nice*. There may be a hint of a suicidal tendency in "God Only Knows." At the very least there is disillusionment. There is a note of hope, in "I'm Waiting for the Day," but it's mixed with uncertainty: love belongs firmly in the past or the future, it cannot be now.

The beach is a liminal state, intermediate between the concrete and tarmac (and the little deuce coupe) of solid land and the rigours and hazards of the ocean wave. The future tense predominates: "We'll find a place in the sun where everyone can have "fun," "Beaches in Mind"). There is nothing sadder than that line.

It seems that both Ted Deerhurst and Brian Wilson suffered from nostalgia for the future. What, to them, seems difficult to the point of impossible is achieving a sense of living and being in the present moment. The Wilson oeuvre, taken as a whole, sounds like a critique of a metaphysics of presence which may be (both in the affirmation and the repudiation) the distinctive note of sixties utopianism. There is a *Waiting for Godot*-esque mood in all the talk of how good it is going to be at some point further down the road: "We'll all be planning out a route we're going to take real soon. We're waxing down our surfboards, we can't wait for June."

Perhaps Brian Wilson was preoccupied above all by inauthenticity. It wasn't just that the Beach Boys couldn't surf. The conflict between what they were supposed to be and what they really were became increasingly unbearable to someone like Wilson. Drugs came along to fill the void. Glen Campbell died when I was on the West Coast and I learned that he had played guitar on *Pet Sounds* and had gone on tour with the band. It struck me that his brand of wistful, melancholic yearning is integral to the Beach Boys mentality. Or think of Peggy Sue, for example: "how my heart yearns for you." Presumably unrequited.

But there remained the hope.

Ted would have understood and appreciated all that. They were singing his song. Just take out Peggy Sue and insert Heather Thomas. Or Deya'. Or Margaret. Or, above all, Lola. Whatever the exact circumstances of his death, I can't help but feel that he died afflicted by disappointment. Greg Huglin reckoned he would still have been dissatisfied even if he had, *per impossibile*, made world champion. It's plausible.

It wasn't just his dream of the "perfect wave" and (his own fond idea) the "perfect woman" that were bound to run into a reef. He wanted to be "one of the boys" and attain some kind of union with his immediate environment, but he discovered that the beach was the unforgiving realm of a reborn feudalism. Like the lonely swain of some courtly romance, he revered and looked up to a new dominant semi-sublime class of "living legends" and archetypal bikini-clad beauty. But one to which he could never himself belong. Ted was a dreamer. When he died, a little of the dream of the beach as the promised land of freedom drowned alongside him.

At the end of *The Order of Things*, Michel Foucault says that the very concept of the human is doomed to disappear shortly, "like a face drawn in sand at the edge of the sea." The tide comes in and the tide goes out and everything can begin once again. Draw the face one more time. An exercise in eternal recurrence. As Blackie said, "Everything comes back–like flares and vinyl records." Ted lived in this twilight zone between earth and ocean, seeing a world in a grain of sand and listening to the sound of the mighty waters rolling ever more.

37

What would really have helped is if I could have taken Ted to a psychoanalyst. He might have benefited from having a proper Freudian to check him out and put his powers of sublimation to the test, discern the contours of his infantile trauma and track them through to assorted syndromes and neuroses. Or maybe a psychiatrist or clinical psychologist, adept at detecting obsessional tendencies and compulsions. Maybe he was suffering from a disorder of some kind, maybe he could be fixed. A touch of aristophobia. Combined with more than a dash of hydrophilia. Maybe Wilhelm Reich had come up with a surfing equivalent of the orgasmatron (or "orgone accumulator")–but then I guess that was Hawaii.

I did once make a discreet suggestion along these lines, after I'd known him for a few years, something like, "Do you ever think of getting help?" We were sitting on our boards at Jocko's. No visible waves as such. But the sun was shining and the sea was blue and we were happy enough bobbing about, eyeing the horizon.

"You think I'm mad, don't you?" He gave a mad laugh.

"Not exactly, no. Well, OK, maybe just a bit."

"I'm normal," he said. "Everyone else is mad." He paused for a while, having provided what seemed to me like a text-book definition of madness, and reflected. "You know, maybe

I really should go and see a psychoanalyst. They could use me as a kind of barometer by which to judge the general population."

Oddly enough, around the same time I met Ted, I happened to bump into an actual psychiatrist in Haleiwa. In a non-clinical context: in fact, in the Coffee Gallery. She and I somehow fell into conversation and she told me she specialized in treating depression. I was incredulous, verging on outraged. "What! Here in Hawaii? How is that even possible?" Specializing in depression in Hawaii seemed to be about as improbable as being a surfing correspondent in England. This was back in my naive utopian youth when I still thought of Hawaii as some kind of terrestrial paradise. Something to do with palm trees and coconuts and pineapples and blue skies and white sands and sultry breezes and—above all—perfect waves. Also, conceivably, people like her. Her name was Sun and she was an indecipherable mix of East and West.

"Where do you come from?" she replied.

"England," I said.

"England!" said she, in a dreamy kind of way. "You're so lucky." Another of her mystifying, seemingly absurd statements. Perhaps she was actually a patient rather than one of the doctors in some lunatic asylum.

"How do you work that out?" I had just flown thousands of miles to get away from England in the middle of winter and come here.

"Because," she said, "in England you can be miserable and nobody minds. They expect you to be miserable."

On account of my being so skeptical about what she did, she ended up taking me on a brief tour of her clinic in Kahuku, which was beyond Turtle Bay, and therefore not North Shore at all, but rather the East Shore, which everyone referred to as the Windward Side. I had to concede in the end that she had a serious job and depression in Hawaii was real.

Sun said, "Exactly the same ratio of the population are depressed in Hawaii as anywhere else. Except here it's worse."

"But at least you have better weather here. And better waves."

"It's all to do with expectations," she explained. "In Hawaii you're supposed to be happy. We're the 'Happy Isles'. Stupid idea, but it's stuck. So everybody thinks they ought to be happy and when they're not they feel guilty about it on top. So you get a double dose."

She hadn't finished either. Turned out it was more like a triple than a double. "And if you consider that Hawaii is part of America, where you're supposed to be prosperous too, then if you're broke as well as depressed then you're really in trouble." It was the dark side of Hawaii. You won't find it in any tourist brochure but it's there. North Shore neurosis. What they call "rock fever."

It was like a remote control analysis of a certain surf-obsessed fugitive viscount. I'm not saying Ted was depressed. He had highs and lows like everyone else. And he always got back on his horse. But he felt the weight of expectations to an inordinate degree. The pressure to achieve. Whether from his own family back in England or from his adopted family, the tribe of nomads in shorts or wetsuits. He had given up one value system for another but found himself wandering alone in a no man's land somewhere in-between. Ted was a victim of romantic anomie, that rule-free uprootedness that Emile

Durkheim described as "the infinity of dreams." A condition that could, in certain circumstances, lead in the direction of suicide.

There was something poetically appropriate about filming *Jurassic Park* in Hawaii (one scene in particular was shot up in the hills above the psychiatric clinic). The islands had a paleolithic quality which had nothing to do with their volcanic origin. Everyone who lived there was fighting out a primeval struggle for survival. It was a harsh, brutal environment, masked by beauty, in which there would always be winners and losers. In the years after Ted's death, they filmed *Lost* on the North Shore and on the Windward Side. I binge-watched whole seasons while staying in a house on Waimea Bay. And I found myself yelling (pointlessly) at characters on the screen, "But you can't be 'lost'–if you go a hundred yards up that stretch of beach, the Coffee Gallery is right there!"

But of course you can always be lost, whether you're in Hawaii or anywhere else. With or without the Coffee Gallery. As if you had survived a plane crash somewhere in the middle of the Pacific and afterwards nothing in the entire world made much sense. You could be lost, and then you would seek, and ultimately you would find.

38.

Thanks to Ted, I got to go to Femme Nu, in downtown Honolulu. I guess I might not have gone otherwise. You can call it—as it was then known—an "exotic dance" club. Or a "pole-dancing venue." Or just plain old "strip joint." I'm not going to argue with you. I haven't seen many places like it. I was once in Paris looking for the so-called Sex Museum (or "Musée de l'érotisme"). They were supposed to have an exhibition connected to the (Soccer) World Cup, back in 1998, which I happened to be reporting on. "Yes, this is the place," said a woman at the door and I was shoved into a room where a number of women were kicking a ball about and wearing, then not wearing, football kit. One woman was the referee, dressed in black shorts and black shirt with a whistle round her neck. Soon all that was left was the whistle. I was also threatened with having to pay eighty euros for an orange juice before I managed to slip out on a tide of receding Scotsmen.

Femme Nu was a bit like that. I worried about one thing. The spelling. It really ought to have the feminine "e" on the end of "Nu" surely? Naked or not, you couldn't neglect grammar. You had to have agreement between noun and adjective otherwise it was sheer anarchy. OK there was one other thing: the pronunciation. It ought to be (if we want to be correct about it) "fam new" (very approximately). As it was I had to adjust to the local parlance and say "Fem noo," if I wanted to be understood. Minor details, I know, but I thought it was important to get these things right.

Ted, indifferent as he was to pronunciation and grammatical niceties, was concerned with other sorts of details. They had to be just right too. A certain anatomical grammar. In that late-night emergency phone call from Hawaii, Ted knew I didn't believe in his concept of the perfect woman because we had already had a long conversation on the subject. We were sitting at one of those benches in front of the Coffee Gallery in Haleiwa at the time. Looking out over the North Shore Market Place. We were supposed to be talking about surfing. It was what I was getting paid for, being a "surfing correspondent" at the time. I was not a girlfriend correspondent or anything like it. But Ted's insight was that, at some level, everything was connected to surfing. His war games, for example. Strategy was important, for one thing. And then romance, of course, how could that not affect the way you surfed? Maybe, as he argued from the very beginning, Freud had it all wrong, and the key to becoming the Perfect Surfer was to have a Perfect Surfer Girl right alongside you. But of course I had to go and be devil's advocate.

"Show me the perfect guy and I will show you the perfect woman," I said, slamming down my glass of iced latte.

Being Ted, he didn't see that as an irony-laced rhetorical challenge, he thought I really wanted to know what a perfect guy would look like. "I guess he would be something like a combination of Kelly Slater and Winston Churchill," he said. Slater had not only won the first US Excalibur contest in 1986 but had risen, in the '90s, to become the hottest young surfer in the world. Churchill was synonymous (in Ted's mind) with Ted himself.

"OK," said I, giving way on this point. "So what would your perfect woman look like then?" Again I was being skeptical. I thought this would floor old Ted. As usual I was wrong.

"I know exactly what she would look like," he replied smugly, as if he already had perfect intimate knowledge of the perfect woman. Ted was like the Socrates of surfing: he had a mystic Idea or Form of the Woman inscribed in his brain, as if he had met her in a previous life. "One day you'll see."

"You're a dreamer," I said.

"She is real, I know it."

"Even if she is real," I said, trying to meet him halfway, "surely you are narrowing down your options very severely." I tried reasoning with him. "Isn't it better just to see what happens and not walk around with an image of perfection in your head? You're automatically ruling out 99.9% of the female half of the human race. You're looking at a world of pain. Why make life difficult for yourself?" And other such reasonable and sensible remarks.

But Ted remained unconvinced. Or, to turn it around, convinced. It was all clear in his mind. He would not swerve from the path. The quest for the unattainable must go on. It was such a clear "picture in his head" (as Crammie said) that he even tried to recruit Greg Huglin to shoot it, with Ted alongside the Perfect Woman as she walked down the street in very high heels: only they never did manage to find the right candidate to fill those highly improbable shoes. You could almost say that Ted was constantly auditioning. Carmel, Dick Hoole's ex, reckoned that sexual obsession was "the lowest level of the kundalini." But there was always more to it than that in Ted's case. Maybe he was mad, but maybe also there was something of the poet about Ted, the utopian, the lyrical visionary. He put me in mind of the poet Baudelaire, and not just because of the green hair that both had at different times. "There," Baudelaire wrote in his dreamy "L'invitation au voyage," "everything is order and beauty, luxury, tranquility and pleasure." The last word that I have translated by "pleasure" is in fact "volupté": more literally, voluptuousness. And voluptuousness was definitely on the menu at Femme Nu.

I am fast-forwarding a year or so after this conversation. And returning to the scene of the nightclub in downtown Honolulu. When he invited me over to meet her (reversing the charges), I didn't believe he had really found the perfect woman, but I was due to go to Hawaii in the summer anyway to write a travel article. Which is when Ted drove us both from the North Shore down to Honolulu, parked the car, and led the way into Femme Nu. None of the labels I've offered above are really accurate. In Ted's mind, this place was more like Xanadu, an immense "stately pleasure dome." Here at last was order, beauty, luxury, tranquility and pleasure. In reality there was some kind of music going on and a measure of noise, but none of that seemed very significant. There were spot lights in one portion of the club too, illuminating the platform that occupied a central area, where several women were dancing. There were a lot of men there too, sitting below the platform, gazing intently at the women, who were in varying degrees of undress.

The scene reminded me a lot of the day before finals at the University Library (where I had been not so long before) when undergraduates who had not really worked hard enough were suddenly impelled to study overtime and were focusing on their textbooks so that they would remember everything the next day when they would be tested on their knowledge. At Femme Nu, all the guys were majoring in anatomy. They were a bit rusty and they needed to go over the details one last time so it would be clearly fixed in their mind's eye for future reference. They wanted to graduate cum laude. They were focused. I guess the main difference was that they would fork out dollar bills of various denominations and shove them into the band that each of the dancers wore around their leg. Like a tip, rewarding (or soliciting) special attention.

Lola wasn't on stage though. She didn't need to be. She was sitting with us in a booth away from the bright lights. We were in shadow, bathed only in a discreet glow. Hence I only ever saw her in outline—the silhouette of Lola. Even though she was naked, many of the details were lost to me. Nor, to be honest, did we have much of a conversation. Ted introduced me and I said hi to her. But she was busy at the time, nuzzling Ted's neck and whispering in his ear. She was sitting on his lap. She had her arms around him. She was pressing her breasts into his face. Ted had to pull his face away from her in order to speak. Not that he was saying that much as I recall. She wasn't small, Lola. Probably around Ted's height, 5' 9." Long legs. And even in the darkness it was obvious that she was blonde. Like a lighthouse, lit up even at night, but in her case more liable to sink than save wandering sailors in the darkness. I guessed mainland, probably West Coast, in origin. But, as I say, we didn't have a whole lot of conversation, she and I, and not enough to clarify these matters.

Finally Lola got up, gave me a nod in passing, and strolled away down the aisle to go about her business. I could discern the fundamentals of her geometry, picked out by the pool of light. The basic architecture.

"Was I right?" said Ted, unable to keep a note of triumph out of his voice.

"You were right," I had to admit. "She is perfect." You could argue (and some did) that Ted must have been struggling with his "feminine side" and therefore resorted to hyping up his masculinity. It was a theory. But the fact is that Lola (aka "Lois" and "Lulu," and I imagine her real name was something else again) was Ted's archetype, finally–Heather Thomas and Margaret Dupré and Susan and Debbie all rolled into one, the word made flesh. A myth that happened to be real. She was like a miracle, even if I suspected there could have been some element of bio-engineering involved. A fantasy woman who had sprung to life.

"She loves me, you know."

"I'm not saying she doesn't," I said, turning back to Ted. "But do you think it could have anything to do with the twenty-dollar bills you kept tucking into that little band on her leg?"

"Nope," he said, unmoved. It was impossible to catch him out: he reminded me of certain philosophers who have their entire systems fully articulated in their heads. Unshakeable. Evangelical in his faith. "I have to do that. Otherwise the management will give her a hard time. She has to appear to be doing business, you see." Ted explained patiently, as if speaking to an idiot. "The reality is she really does love me. But we have to keep up appearances. As if I was just another customer. They don't want her going off-piste."

"No, of course not," I said.

Ted sighed. "True love at last."

He told me how it had happened. He had been work-ing with a photographer called Hank. Hank was a regular at Femme Nu and had invited Ted along. Ted had never been there before and thought it would be an interesting experi-ence. And then he had seen Lola, for the first time, and been instantly smitten (and vice versa, he assured me). Thus he became a regular visitor, going there every day after class in Honolulu. "This the real thing," he said. Even in the darkness I could see him smile broadly. He had the awestruck look of a man who has seen God.

"And now you've found the perfect woman there is noth-ing to prevent you from becoming surfing champion of the world, right?"

"Exactly," he said.

I was being ironic.

He wasn't.

Irony was the product of a cynical, jaded sense that noth-ing ever quite lived up to the hype. To Ted's way of thinking, everything was now perfect, it had always been supposed to be like this, and now it finally was, the remaining parts of the puzzle slotting neatly into place. Irony vanquished. Quest complete. Mission accomplished.

Except I suppose for one small thing. Ted had already uttered the word. The "management."

Ted dropped me off at the airport in his beaten-up old Porsche. His last words were, "It's the real thing." He didn't have to say what he was talking about.

39.

"I've become really good friends with the Hawaiians," Ted said in one of his last interviews in *The Surfer's Path*, dating from the mid-90s. "I really love the Hawaiian people. I love their friendly attitude." He was not being naïve. Many Hawaiians fully reciprocated the sentiment. The Bustin' Down the Door era was over. Wounds had (by and large) healed. Aloha was, once again, imaginable.

But, all the same, Ted and Lola were bound to incur the wrath of "the management." The management, it turned out, was none other than his old adversary Pit Bull (honorary Hawaiian) and associates (or gang, whatever). He either owned Femme Nu or had a stake in it or was somewhere shadily behind it. But not very far behind. He kept a close eye on everything that occurred within his small empire. Including the women who performed there. Which naturally included Lola. There were different accounts of the relationship between them. Some maintained that Lola was his "girlfriend." Others said that it was strictly business. The truth was it didn't make that much difference to someone like Pit Bull. It was all one. He needed control over his employees. *Coercive* control, if necessary. And Lola was now officially out of control. She was running around town with this English milord dude. And he was paying her but Pit Bull wasn't getting his cut, so something would have to be done about it.

A certain amount of time went by and then, one day, Ted heard a knock on his door. I was back in Hawaii and he was telling me about this shortly afterwards. He was still looking a little pale and shakey. We were in d'Amicos–a hundred yards up the Kamehameha highway from Sunset–having a pizza. He wasn't all that hungry and was merely poking at his Napolitana. Normally he would be shovelling it in. His mind wasn't on the job.

"What's up?" I said. Which is when he told me the whole story.

The two guys had been perfectly polite. And that is what made the whole thing so terrifying. You didn't encounter politeness all that often, not on the North Shore. It was a real rarity. And, said Ted, they were "dressed in suits." By which I think he meant that they were wearing long pants (also rare) and probably short-sleeved shirts. Not t-shirts. They meant business. No weapons were produced either. And yet every word had the force of a sawn-off shotgun behind it. They were big guys, the size of sumo wrestlers, but fit-looking, in shape. Looked like they worked out. And one of them smiled a lot too. Ted never did find out what their names were. Didn't think to ask.

But they knew his name all right. "Hello, Ted," they said. "Or should we say Lord Ted?" They were some kind of "security," but on an island where security made you feel anything but secure.

Ted grinned a nervous sort of grin. "'Ted' will be just fine," he said.

They also knew exactly where he lived, needless to say. Because they had knocked on the door of no. 100, East Kuilima. Ted's little condo. It's up the stairs. The place downstairs is another number. So it was half a house. Nothing imposing. Modest, but a roof over his head. Space to park his boards and a spare pair of shorts. And these two guys had come up the stairs and knocked on his door and were standing politely on the porch. Ted had opened the door but was standing on his side of the threshold. They never crossed the threshold either. They did not venture into Ted territory. They remained politely conversing from their side of the line. Two big smiling guys. Or rather only one of them smiled. He did all the speaking too. The other guy just stood there sullenly, not really doing anything. Not yet anyway. He was only an implication, but a damn big heavy one.

There was some exchange to do with how there was a big swell coming. In Hawaii there always was either a big swell coming or a bunch of guys saying that it was. Ted agreed that it certainly was coming.

"We hear you're a good surfer, Ted," said the smiler.

Ted tried to be modest, even though terrified. "Well, not bad," he said.

"Way we hear it, you could be champion, one day."

"One of these days maybe," he said. He wasn't about to argue with that.

Then they got to the crux of it. "Well, look here, Ted, how do you think it would be if you had to surf on just one leg? Do you think you would surf as good then?"

Ted could envisage it all too easily. He imagined that they would probably blow a hole through his leg with a shotgun and it would have to be amputated, something like that. Probably not a machete. That was too much hands-on. They weren't literally going to chop his leg off, but it would amount to the same thing. He gulped and managed to croak a reply. "I think that would be hard," he said.

The guy had a good chuckle at that. "Oh, come on, Ted," he said, striking a cheerful, upbeat note and slapping him on the shoulder. "It wouldn't be all that bad. A challenge, yes. But you'd adapt. These new artificial legs they have these days, they're better than your actual leg. Yeah, maybe you'd be even better with just one leg. Don't you think?"

Ted said nothing. He had run out of words. His throat was dry.

"Or..." said the guy. Long pause. "OR," ramming the point home with a raised finger and upper case just in case Ted was not getting it, even though he clearly was getting it, "you could just leave Lola alone."

"Lola," said Ted.

"The blonde. She's not yours, brah. So you should stop seeing her, stop fooling around with her, stop driving her in your car, stop giving her presents. Stop fucking her. Because if you're fucking Lola you're fucking Pit Bull."

Ted said nothing. The thought was hideous.

"Just stop. Or you could try surfing on one leg. Which would you prefer?"

Ted managed to come out with a line that has stuck solidly in my mind. "It's her loss," he said. Good line. That was clear then. The two guys were satisfied with that line. Anyone would be. Anyone other than Ted that is.

"Yeah, I guess she's going to be real sad for a while. But don't you worry, we'll look after Lola. She'll be OK." Like they really cared.

They said a polite farewell to Ted and then they politely went back down the stairs and politely got into their car and politely drove away. There was no violence at all. Ted was not roughed up. No blood was spilt. No injuries were incurred. And yet the threat of all that happening, right up to and including the removal of a limb, was abundantly clear in Ted's mind.

Ted had worked it all out. He always had it all worked out. "Lola told Pit Bull she was leaving him for me and he couldn't take that so he sends in the heavies. It's jealousy pure and simple. Guy like Pit Bull, he just can't stand the heat."

I nodded sympathetically while demolishing my pizza.

"But you want to know the really hard thing about all this?" he said to me, chasing an olive around his plate.

"It all sounds pretty damn hard to me," I said.

"We were going to get married," Ted said.

"What!?" I nearly choked on an olive. I guess I shouldn't have been so amazed. I hadn't taken the whole thing seriously enough. She was only a chance encounter in a nightclub, I thought—a passing fancy. To Ted it was all deadly serious. She was the perfect woman after all. The real thing.

"Of course," he said. "We were going to get married right here on Oahu. Then she wanted to come to England to meet my family and all that." I could envisage the scene. She would have to put some clothes on of course. But Bill would probably be enchanted. He loved dancers too. Maybe even Mimi would approve. As usual, Ted had it all worked out.

And now it was all over. "This is going to break her heart," he said. "She really did love me, you know." But he could never see Lola again. Not if he wanted to surf on two legs rather than just the one. "Maybe it's for the best. I have law exams coming up soon. I really ought to concentrate on that."

Exactly what I would say in his shoes. The fact is that I had been in a similar position myself. Not over a woman of course. But I had been warned off and I had stayed warned off. If I wanted to continue to live and work on the North Shore I had to behave and abide by the rules and not upset anybody. We all understood the system. And the same applied to Ted. He had received the warning and so he would stay warned off. Or would he? There was a big fat "OR," as the two guys had said.

And what we know of Ted is that he would always get back on his horse. Mimi had taught him to. It was practically in his DNA.

40.

I wrote Ted's obituary. I didn't see how he died. I was back in England, Ted was in Hawaii. I only heard about it from the newspaper. The section editor phoned me up, said how they'd heard on the wire that this guy Lord Ted had died and didn't I know him and could I write the obituary?

I had no idea that Ted had even been ill. I thought he had fully recovered. But, I thought, maybe his injuries had taken their toll. I called a few people and nobody really knew how he had died. Everyone could remember times when Ted *should* have died. That time at Haleiwa, for example, when the surf was so huge that the women's pro contest had been called off, and Ken Bradshaw, Randy Rarick and Ian Cairns all stoutly refused to go out. And Ted went out anyway. Like the Charge of the Light Brigade, as Shaun Tomson would have said. Got massacred, three times over, massive sets right on his head. His board comes in to shore, without him. People are calling for the lifeguards. But then he swims in, grabs his board and paddles right back out again. Classic Ted.

You couldn't find a lot of people in Hawaii who were too surprised that he was dead. Some expressed surprise that he had lived as long as he did. In England the archivist of the Coventry family said that there was a "curse" on the name of Deerhurst because so many sons had pre-deceased their fathers.

Did Ted himself have some presentiment of impending doom? Margaret Dupré's daughter, India, kept a "memory book" in which she invited thoughts or sketches from others. In it, less than a year before he died, at the grand old age of thirty-nine, Ted had written, "Life is short–don't waste it." Did he know he wasn't going to make it this time? Maybe. But the point about an obituary is it's not like an inquest. It's about the life not the death.

This is what I wrote, shortly after October 4, 1997:

Edward George William Omar Coventry, surfer: born 24 September 1957; styled Viscount Deerhurst since birth; died North Shore, Oahu, Hawaii 4 October 1997.

Ted Deerhurst was a serious surfer. But being born the son of the Earl of Coventry and thereby acquiring the nickname of "Lord Ted" in surfing circles, he had his work cut out convincing the cognoscenti that he was anything other than a playboy. Sleeping in a beaten-up old car, being broke for long periods and having an American mother probably helped. His high point was reaching the semi-finals of the Smirnoff at big Sunset Beach in 1978. But even though he never hit the top 100 in the professional rankings, he was, in many ways, the most persistent and committed performer on the world circuit.

He had to be: Deerhurst always surfed his heart out in every contest he competed in and he was nearly always trounced. He was a hero of never-say-die optimism. He was the only surfer who read history between heats (his idol was Winston Churchill). Every now and then he would be cast down after another crushing defeat, but he would invariably bounce back. When he was seven, his horse threw him and stomped on him and his mother just put him straight back in the saddle: "I guess I've been getting back on that horse ever since," he said.

One December in Hawaii, at the end of his worst-ever tour, he discovered he had slid down the ladder from 189 to 231st in the world. It was the same year that Martin Potter, another Brit, took the world championship. Anyone else would have thrown in the towel—not Deerhurst though. While admitting he didn't have a realistic shot at the title, he still came up with the ingenious aim of winning the Most Improved Surfer of the Year award: he figured he would only have to jump up to around a hundred or so from his current lowly position to achieve the fastest rise in the history of pro surfing. Another time he switched to snowboarding with the famous last words, "At least you can't drown up a mountain." He spent the next six months in hospital.

Although he once surfed, as an amateur, for England, Deerhurst was a footloose citizen of the surf who lived at different times in Australia, California and finally on the North Shore of Hawaii, where the mightiest waves in the world come to die every winter and generally take a few surfers with them. He masqueraded as a university student, but whenever the surf was up school was out. He became an adept of big-wave conditions and once described surfing a twenty-foot wave at Waimea Bay as being like "jumping off a three-storey house— and then having the house chase you down the street." His ultimate dream was of finding sponsors in Britain to fund the equipment for tow-in surfing in thirty-foot plus waves.

Even though he was approaching forty he still competed. He speculated that the lack of a long-term girlfriend to accompany him on his travels might have been holding him back. He tried to rectify matters by falling in love with an exotic dancer in a nightclub in Honolulu, but the extremely jealous gangster who was her boyfriend stood in the way of his plans.

Ted Deerhurst was an altruist among surfers. He set up the Excalibur Foundation (named after the boards he shaped with their distinctive sword logo) to enable handicapped and underprivileged kids to go surfing. Towards the end of his life, he was proud to have become a fully integrated member of the Hawaiian community and was in the forefront of the battle to prevent overdevelopment of the North Shore. The hard-to-impress locals treated him with respect and called him "brother."

Many of them gathered to paddle out at Sunset Beach—the scene of his greatest triumph—in eight-to-ten feet surf and sprinkle his ashes upon the waves. "He wasn't on the fringe of surfing," said Michael Willis, fellow surfer and shaper, "he was right at the heart."

The motto of Excalibur was "Sharing the spirit of surfing." Ted Deerhurst was the energetic embodiment of that ideal.

I had spoken on the phone to Michael Willis (one half of the "Willis Bros" twins, creators of the Phazer-bottom board), who had lived for many years on the North Shore. He had told me about the paddle-out. Ted had been cremated and his ashes scattered upon the water, as was the convention in Hawaii (he gets a name-check on Bill's tombstone back in England:

In Memory of his beloved only son
TED
Viscount Deerhurst
Born 1957 Died 1997

At the base of the stone, covered in moss and lichen, barely visible, is a line from Elizabeth Barrett Browning's sonnet, "How Shall I Love Thee?": *And if God choose I shall but love thee better after death*). The fact that someone had just dropped dead didn't mystify Michael Willis at all. People were always dying on the North Shore, many prematurely. Usually by drowning. Ted had always done things just a little bit differently. But Michael wasn't too sure exactly what had happened. To him it didn't even matter that much. You were either alive or you were dead, and how you made the transition from one to the other was a matter of indifference.

"Be cool, brah," was the kind of response I tended to get whenever I tried to find out exactly what had happened. Ted was immortal anyway, his memory would never die, and so on. An attitude that finally drove me mad. As Popeye would say, I can't stands no more. In England I was a mild-mannered, easy-going, broadly skeptical kind of citizen. But Hawaiian haziness and the code of omertà turned me into a monster of fact-checking precision. I was as persistent and stubborn as Ted himself, except that I was hanging around the records offices of the Honolulu Police HQ and the Hawaii Health Department. It wasn't extracting a sword, more getting blood out of a stone. And the more you check the facts about what really happened to Ted, the more the yawning gaps and contradictions become apparent. It took me another twenty years to really fathom it out.

There was the tantalising question of "Lola." Whatever her real name might be. I scoured Oahu, town and country, looking for her. What had become of her? Where was she living now? How much did she know? After Ted died, she simply vanished. Ted had cried out for more attention, more photographs, more column inches. Lola didn't want to be found. She wasn't available for interview. Which is exactly what convinced me that she must know something. That and the fact that when I mentioned her name, in conjunction with the words "Femme Nu," her old friends tended to clam up. The new Femme Nu club knew nothing. Maybe, some suggested, she had gone back to the mainland. Assuming, that is, she was still alive. Perhaps she had taken her secrets to the grave.

There remain several conflicting accounts of Ted's final days. The English photographer Alex Williams wondered if it could have been suicide. He recalled two suicides he had known. One guy took the sleeping-in-a-car approach to its logical conclusion, with the aid of a hosepipe connected to the exhaust. Then there was the Geordie surfer Nigel Veitch, who changed his name to plain Veitch because he thought the "Nigel" was holding him back. It was uncool. He invested a huge amount in the pro tour on the strength of promised backing from Newcastle Brown Ale. Then they pulled out. He cancelled all debts by throwing himself off the cliffs at Tynemouth.

But Ted's death–this much is clear–was not voluntary or consensual. It was no "choking game"-style accident.

Of course there is Rabbit Bartholomew's idea, that Ted drowned while surfing at Sunset. Wiped out in the tube and never came up. Nice idea. Fed to him, apparently, by Bernie Baker, the great North Shore oracle. A lot of people thought that. Alex Williams thought that is what had happened to him too, although he also thought the drowning was, if not willed and embraced, then at least accepted and conceded. He showed me a board (a Sunset-dedicated 7' 4"), tucked away in a barn on his farm in Devon, shaped by Ted, on which he had scribbled the following enigmatic message (inscribed on the wooden section known as the "stringer"): "The door is open." Could that be something to do with crossing the threshold into the great beyond? I thought it was more a reference to Bustin' Down the Door: the door–to pro surfing–had been opened, all you had to do was walk through it. More optimistic than apocalyptic.

At the other end of the spectrum, the idea got around that he had died in a hotel room somewhere. Some thought he must have OD'd, just as Andy Irons would do a few years later. Again, way off the mark. The most surreal theory I came across was that Ted (the son of a would-be 007 after all) was a British secret agent (spying on Hawaii?) and had been bumped off by the KGB or a Colombian cartel. "Pro surfer" would be a great cover story for his global exploits. But there were other interpretations that were closer to the truth.

Here is one I had direct from a lawyer. Surely he ought to know?

There was one big silver lining (according to the legal eagle point of view). Bill and Ted. Ted and Bill. After everything they had been through, beyond all the drama and the heartache, they were finally reunited. Ted was well again, looking like his old self. He was out of the cage. And Bill was happier than he had ever been. Ted flew back to England for Bill's marriage to Rachel Wynne in 1992. He had a haircut and wore a suit. And he behaved well at the wedding. Perhaps Bill had expected more outrageous. And Rachel liked him too, as did her son Matt. "I'm glad my dad has found someone to make him happy," he said. So all that helped.

He had competed at Pipe in the winter of 1996 (when he wiped out in the first heat). Then, in August of 1997, we find him once more in Europe to compete on the French and Spanish legs of the ASP tour. He was now officially the Oldest Guy on the Tour. Which he was secretly quite pleased about. He went back to where I first met him, Lacanau and Biarritz and Hossegor. He still didn't get through the qualifying rounds but at least now he had an excuse of sorts. Old age. Afterwards he returned to England one last time. He stayed at Croome for a week shortly before his fortieth birthday. He was fit again. Insisted on sleeping on the floor. Four-posters galore and he wanted a futon or a yoga mat. Better for the posture. Rachel, Bill's wife, Countess of Coventry, remembers it because she made some passing crack about his upcoming birthday, something like, "You'll be forty soon–you'll have to get a proper job," or "you'll have to grow up finally." And Ted overreacted, like she had said something deeply wounding.

Anyone else would have laughed it off. But Ted burst out, "I don't want to get old!" The idea of turning forty filled Ted with anxiety. He had been a Peter Pan character for so long, he wanted to stay that way. Despite which, they all got along just fine.

Bill and Ted would meet one more time at Bill's club in London, just off Pall Mall. Gentlemen only. Hushed and exclusive. A place of immense restfulness and deep armchairs and newspapers and waiters serving drinks on silver trays. In another time and place, there might have been a more emotional scene, with hugs and tears, but not here, not now. They spoke quietly, almost in whispers. They sat in adjacent chairs, the thickness of two ample and comfortable arms between them.

"Edward," Bill said, putting his glass down and turning to look at his son. He is inches taller than Ted but it doesn't matter since they are sitting down. These days he has a grey beard. Not so much the old 007 look: 007 retired. More Captain Haddock. He almost never called him Edward, it was always Ted. But just this once. "We can't go back and change things, can we? I wish we could. I'd do everything differently if I had a second bite at life. But it's not too late to change, is it?"

"No, I suppose not." Ted had no idea what his father was talking about.

"What I mean to say is," Bill said, stumbling and stuttering. "I'm a bit of a failure as a dad. Nobody ever told me how to do it. I just thought I knew. But I was wrong."

Ted had never heard his father apologise for anything before. He didn't know what to say.

"Maybe it had something to do with losing my own father when I was so young. I didn't want to lose you too. So I held on to you too tight. I should have let you do what it was you wanted to do, not try to lay down the law. Overdoing it. Trying too hard."

"Father," said Ted, choking up, "you're the perfect father. You always have been. I'm the problem. I can see that now. I was a bad son." He didn't call him Bill for a change, he called him "Father."

"I was a bad father."

"I'm going to try to be a better son in the future. I'll do whatever you want me to do."

"Ted, all I want is for you to be happy. I…"

Ted reached out his hand and held his father's arm.

"I want you to know that you are no longer a stranger to me. I mean, legally. You are my son and heir again. I've asked our solicitor to make all the arrangements."

"I love you, father," said Ted. It was the kind of language that was not heard very often in the precincts of a gentleman's club in London. A word–"love"–Ted and Bill had never uttered to one another before.

"God bless you, Teddy," said Bill, his eyes welling up. It was his pet name for Ted when he was a kid, one that he hadn't used in so many years.

Ted was getting up to leave. Then he stopped. "Hey, I nearly forgot. I've got something for you in here." He dug around in his bag and pulled out a wooden dolphin he had brought all the way from Hawaii. He had had it carved especially. The dorsal fin was broken, hanging down over the dolphin's back. "I wanted to give you this, but look, it's broken."

Bill took it. "No, it isn't," he said.

They embraced (again, something they had not often done). But only on the street outside the club. It was probably prohibited inside. They didn't want to offend against the rules. Ted promised that he would return to England and take up his seat in the House of Lords when and if his father died. "I just pray that won't be for many years yet."

Bill laughed. "Don't have to worry about that," he said. "There's life in the old dog yet."

This is the sequence of events that the lawyer recounted to me. The timeline. It's a long way home for Ted, even if it's a journey he's done many times before. Ted takes a taxi to Heathrow. Gets stuck in traffic. One hour. Sitting around at the airport and queuing up for security—another two hours. Finally the Air New Zealand flight. He flies economy of course, keeping costs down. Eleven hours to Los Angeles. Then he deplanes, goes through immigration, another hour. Finally back on another plane for the hop over the Pacific to Hawaii. It's quite a big hop though. Another five and a half hours. Hanging around in baggage reclaim. Out into the clear Hawaiian air again. So much warmer here than England, but the smells are so different too. Already the sweet smell of pineapple and coconut, even at the airport. Airport car park, pick up Porsche. Drive back to Turtle Bay, H1, H2, and at last the Kamehameha highway back through Haleiwa, past all the familiar spots, the legends. Waimea Bay, Pipeline, Sunset, Velzyland. The last couple of miles that took him all the way up to the turn-off for Turtle Bay, over the rumble strips, then left. Right into East Kuilima. Park right outside no. 100. Then up the stairs and through the door. He's home.

Add it all up: it's not far off twenty-four hours all in all. Not exactly Captain Cook-style, but still a full day. Because of the time difference, it's still the middle of the day before. Hawaii is the yesterday land. You are flying back in time, eleven hours. You arrive the day before, if you think in terms of Greenwich Mean Time. Ted often wondered–and he is bound to wonder this time, is he not, having just turned forty–if he was actually getting younger by flying off to Hawaii again. Turning the clock back. Shaving half a day off his age. Or was it more that he was shaving half a day off his life? He had no idea. But one thing he does know: he is feeling a hell of a lot older than when he set out. Exhausted by all the trooping in and out of cars and trains and planes.

He feels like going to bed. But it's too early for that, it's still only the afternoon. He has a plan. He will go and see Lola later. That will wake him up. And then he will be able to sleep properly through the night. On the other hand, he could really do with some rest and relaxation right now. He can't go surfing. He isn't that stupid. He knows (having tried it once) there's nothing worse than stepping off the plane then paddling out. That way perdition lies. The kind of thing only a pure tourist would do, guaranteed to lead to disaster. Which is why he decides to take a bath. He could have taken a shower. It would have been quicker. But he is in no hurry. He needs to slow down. Take it easy for a short while.

Ted sinks down gratefully into the bath. Looks straight up. There is a skylight right over his head. He can feel all the tension draining out of him. He gazes up at the blue sky, not a cloud in sight. Typical Hawaii, nothing like England. Nothing but blue, with a fringe of golden radiance. The skylight is a porthole window, like the window of a ship, as if the blue could almost be the sea. Blueness all around in Hawaii, wherever you look, up or down. Paradoxically, Ted seems to be falling upwards. He can feel himself drifting dreamily up into the infinite blue over his head. And he has the strange impression that he is floating out of the window above him, surfing on the back of a sunbeam, and as he looks back behind him, he can see himself still there, lying in the bath, broken, bleeding. Except that he–the physical body that was Ted– is slipping, sliding down into the water, below the surface, while he–the spirit that was Ted–is flying free and there are no more limits to what he can do or be. He is finally free.

That is the feel-good version of how Ted died. I've heard something like it a few times. Not that different to Rabbit's idea of his death, except that he drowns in a bath rather than in the ocean. And even this would be a typical Ted move, since drowning like a lot of other surfers would be too obvious, too conventional, and he would be bound to do something different. So let it be the bath. And in fact, so far as I can understand, he did die in the bath. But it wasn't like this. Because the bath didn't even have any water in it. It was an empty bath, apart from Ted. And his blood. Red Ted.

41.

I didn't find out that detail—about the blood—until I spoke to Dan. I won't give his last name because I don't want him to be punished for speaking to me. I don't want what happened to Ted to happen to him. I imagine he feels the same way.

Dan is a big grizzly bear of a guy. About my height, as I discovered when I went to meet him in Hawaii. But a lot wider, more muscular, not fat. He has a nice wife and nice kids too and doesn't want them to be fatherless. He got to know Ted well in his final year or two. They met surfing and ended up playing war games together. Time had rolled on and now it was no longer toy soldiers on the beach but computer games. Dungeons and Dragons and suchlike. If only Call of Duty had been around then they would have been right into it, no doubt. Possibly also Grand Theft Auto. They would also hang out a lot at the glassing shop behind d'Amicos on the Kam highway. And Dan got to meet Lola (he described her convincingly as a "Panzer general California girl"). I believe he saw her with clothes on and in daylight. She came to the North Shore to see Ted from time to time, when he was not going down to Honolulu to see her. So the message from the two guys to stay away from Lola hadn't really taken.

I had a feeling it wouldn't. For one thing, Ted was still in love with Lola and, just as important, he was convinced that she was in love with him (even if, to the casual observer, there was a question mark against this issue: Deya' for one dismissed her as "an opportunist"). Ted had sought and he had found. Maybe he could finally give up seeking. But there was something even stronger than this that meant that Ted would have to ignore the message. His acute sense of justice—and therefore injustice.

All he had done was press pause, briefly, and then resume. Even if he said, "Her loss," on the spur of the moment, it was obvious that as time went by he would soon be saying to himself, "I'm not going to let myself be pushed around. It doesn't matter who her 'boyfriend' is. If she wants to go out with me—or even marry me—that is her decision and not his. I won't stand by and let her suffer" (by which he meant being deprived of his company). He wasn't going to run away. Was he chicken? He would have to stand his ground, no matter what. He had right on his side. And right is might. The flaming sword of justice. Excalibur, the magic sword drawn from the stone. "He would never give up," said Deya', for example, when I mentioned to her what had happened.

And so the romance (whether one-sided or reciprocal) continued. They tried to be discreet about it, but it was bound to come to the attention of the management eventually. People talked, even in Hawaii, especially if it was someone else in the firing line. Ted—just like Rabbit previously—was disrespecting the management. And the management couldn't put up with that.

When Ted went off to Europe at the end of August of 1997, he asked Dan if he would stay at his place and look after the cats. At this point Ted had at least two cats. They were called Ethelred and Guinevere. Arthurian cats. He was always collecting cats. He would pick up cats he found injured at the side of the road or lost and get them fixed and bring them back to life. Ted was a cat rescuer. Dan said he would help out, so he left the place he had been renting in Haleiwa and moved into 100 East Kuilima. Rent-free in exchange for feeding the cats. Good deal. And he was between jobs.

Ted was spotted in Europe. Phil Holden, official surf photographer to the Fosters Surf Masters event at Fistral, saw him north of Biarritz, at Anglet, where he was a wild card, but in good shape and good heart and still not quite getting beyond qualifying. He was sleeping in a van. Planning to go on to Portugal. They talked about doing a shoot together.

When Ted returned at the end of September, he was "stoked," Dan said, on account of being the Oldest Surfer on Tour. It gave him a status he hadn't had before. It was like he had finally been accepted on the circuit. "Never too late," had become his slogan. As he once said to me, "I guess I don't know how to quit. I enjoy it too much. I'm just a surf junkie."

And he had been reconciled with Bill, so that was good too. Everything was working out for him, it seemed. He had Lola, and he was going back to school, at the University of Hawaii. He celebrated his fortieth in Hawaii, with Lola. Maybe they really would get married one day and it wasn't all in his imagination. He would become a lawyer and set the world to rights and they would get married and they would live together happily ever after. And he could still go surfing, even if he didn't become world champion. It had all fallen into place, at just the right time. All the disappointments, all the failures, all the heartache, it had only served to spur him on and make his imminent success all the sweeter.

I knew those were some of the thoughts going through his head because the last letter he wrote to me from Hawaii was all about his plans for the future. He was all worked up about possible overdevelopment of the North Shore and he wanted to prevent that from happening if he could. He was unenthused by a proposed wind farm around Waimea. "Keep the country country": that was his campaign slogan (the North Shore was "country," Honolulu was "town"). Not everyone saw it that way of course, and there were commercial interests that saw huge potential in the wasted green spaces of the North Shore. He wanted me to come over and write a *J'Accuse*-style article about it, denouncing the dark forces that threatened to engulf Hawaii. Or maybe he would write it himself. He was studying journalism, after all (technically, he was taking a BA in Communications and Law).

Ted and Dan would talk politics a lot too. They were, Dan said, "intellectual buddies" as well as fellow surfers. He said that Ted inspired him to go back to school and get the qualifications that would secure him a good job long after Ted had gone.

On Saturday, October 4, 1997, Dan had to go into Honolulu for the day. He said he couldn't exactly remember why. No reason maybe. He just had to go. For the whole day. He went out in the morning and didn't come back till the evening. It would make sense. It took a while driving into Honolulu and back. And then there was the business he had to do while he was in town, that would take time too. The police never asked him about what he was doing in town, though. They didn't ask him about a lot of things, it turned out. Perhaps they knew what had happened all along anyway, so they didn't really need to ask. A chronicle of a death foretold.

When Dan went out that morning he thought Ted wasn't feeling well. "Are you OK?" he said, concerned for his friend. "I'll be fine," said Ted. "Don't worry about me." Almost as if he knew what was coming too. The way Hawaii 5-0 wrote this down was "Deerhurst was having a seizure."

No, he wasn't, Dan said to me. He just didn't look well, that's all. "I never said he was having a seizure."

"Why would the police write that you said that?" I said.

"I don't know," he said.

Dan had not seen the police reports. So far as I can work out the police simply made up around half of what Dan was supposed to have said. Or more like 90%. Not that he said all that much. He thought they were going to arrest him. They were bound to arrest somebody, he thought. Because it looked as if Ted had been murdered. (Sally, Pit Bull's ex, when she heard Dan's account, said flat out, "They killed him"—the "they" in question being indeterminate.)

Dan got back to 100 East Kuilima around 7:30 p.m. The house was quiet. There was no sign of the cats, as if they had fled. The bathroom is almost immediately on your left as you enter. Ted was in the bath, yes. He was naked. And he was dead. But he hadn't been having a peaceful bath and sailed away into the great beyond. Something violent had happened to him. There was no water in the bath for one thing. That struck Dan. So he hadn't been taking a bath. If he'd been running a bath and then died there would be water everywhere.

Ted is face down in the bath with his legs sticking out at the side. He is not breathing. His lips have turned blue and rigor mortis has set in. There is blood in the bath. There is a "contusion" (as it says in the report) to the back of his head. And there are injuries to his face too: cuts on his nose, a black eye. He looks, prima facie, as if he has been beaten up. But, say the police, Ted beat himself up. He "may have hit his head on the bath tub."

Dan calls 911. First a Honolulu Fire Department truck turns up. They pull the "deceased" from the tub and lay him on the floor in the hallway. The Honolulu Police Department team arrive shortly after 8 p.m., followed a minute later by paramedics. There are two officers. One of them interviews Dan while the other looks around the condo. Soon the estate manager turns up and tells him he has to leave the house. His name isn't on the lease so he has to leave. "What, now?" says Dan.

"Right now," says the estate manager. Which comes as a shock to Dan, almost as much as finding Ted dead in the bath. He hadn't planned for this.

"But what about the cats?" says Dan.

"What cats?" says the estate manager. Cats weren't on the lease either, so they didn't exist, from his point of view. Probably Ted wasn't supposed to be looking after cats he had rescued. Maybe if he had been alive he could have argued his case passionately and eloquently. But he wasn't alive any more.

Dan assumed that he was going to be arrested. Somebody must have done this to Ted. He looked like the most likely candidate. He was the last guy (that anyone knew) to see Ted alive and he was the first to find the body. That put him squarely in the frame. He was, at the very least, a suspect. Which is why he could hardly believe it when Hawaii 5-0, who he fully expected to say, "Book 'em, Danno" or words to that effect (such was the classic line of the original Steve McGarrett), said instead, "OK, you can leave now." Just like the estate manager. They were managing the crime scene. They were management too. Except that it wasn't a crime scene. Or was it? There was some ambiguity on this account.

I obtained not just one but two copies of the official police report on the "unattended DOA" of Deerhurst, Edward G. I had a letter with a little coronet on the letterhead saying that I was acting on behalf of the family (this was genuine, by the way, I didn't invent it). On this basis the Archives department at Police HQ in Honolulu had released the 1997 report, but with all the names redacted, even Ted's. Which seemed odd, because I knew it was Ted already, but there was some rule about it. Then I went to get the death certificate from the Health department a few blocks down the street and came back with it a few days later and they gave me another report, this time with Ted's name un-redacted. I found Dan's name in there too, which is how I found Dan.

According to the police report, Dan said a lot of things which he said to me he hadn't said. He said he hadn't had time to say them because they'd only spoken to him briefly and then thrown him out. Nor did they ever track him down to follow up and interview him again. Like they had enough already. They had reached a judgment. Possibly before they even turned up at the house. Here is what "Dan" had to "say":

"As long as I have known Edward, he did not have any enemies. I don't believe anyone was out to get him. He was a nice person."

"Why would I even say that?" said Dan when I spoke to him. "I mean, I might have said he was a nice person. Or nice guy or something. But why would I say that line about having no enemies? That doesn't sound like me." No one had ever asked him if anyone was "out to get him" and he certainly hadn't volunteered the opinion. Everyone had enemies, Dan thought. But the police had to go and insist that Ted was the one guy in Hawaii who didn't.

There was another very weird phrase in the police report too. "Dan" said that "the apartment was locked and intacted."

"What does that mean?" said Dan. *Intacted.* He had no idea. It sounded like police talk to me. And even for police talk it was pretty strange. Possibly just the adjective "intact" turned into a verb, on an analogy with "impact." *Intacted* as the opposite to *impacted*. Ted's wallet, similarly, was "intacted." Idiosyncratic lexical choices.

Says "Dan" in his "statement," "As far as I can see no one appeared to have hurt Edward."

"Bullshit," said Dan. "I never called him Edward. Always Ted."

"I did not see any injuries which was caused by someone." I am quoting the statement again. The atrocious grammar was just like that. On a par with *intacted*. Dan's grammar is perfectly fine. He doesn't use singular verbs for plural nouns. And the fact is: his first thought was that Ted's injuries really had been caused by someone, he just didn't know who. Except that it wasn't him.

Another thing: according to the police, Dan had gone surfing that day. All day. From ten in the morning through till 7:30 in the evening. He hadn't. He had been in Honolulu all day. Not surfing. So far as I could make out, nearly everything about the report was wrong, except that Ted really was dead.

There was one line in the report that I thought would really get Ted's goat: he was described as "an unemployed surfer." Hold on, I thought, his entire career was built around surfing. He was a pro, if anyone was. How was that "unemployed"? A small point, I know, but it felt like–it would have felt like–an insult to Ted. To be honest, the whole report reads like an insult. Ted, apparently, went to Europe "for a vacation." No, he didn't. He was surfing. Surfing was serious. So what if he wasn't cracking million-dollar deals? The police were Hawaiian but they weren't on the wavelength.

Just one more small point about this report. I don't see why any decent officer would write that Mimi, Ted's mother, "was somewhat hysterical when informed" (by phone). Of course she was. She was his mother. Her son was dead. What would you expect? The word "hysterical" seems so unfair to her, as if she was having some kind of nervous breakdown. As if nothing had happened to justify her reaction.

"Evidence Specialists" were called in. Photographs were taken. A diagram of the whole house was prepared. In the order of things, the case had to be turned over to Homicide. *Apparently,* Homicide looked at the initial report. Having brought their investigative powers to bear on the report, they swiftly reached a conclusion. "Natural causes." They said that Ted had "apparently had an epileptic seizure." The word "apparently" comes up a few times in the report. Which is surprising, because it means that you are going on appearances and not getting to the core of what really happened. But maybe he had had a seizure. There was enough in the autopsy to suggest something like this. But nobody wanted to ask what had triggered the seizure, if he'd had one. Perhaps this explains why it is that Dr Yang at the Castle hospital in Honolulu, who had once treated Ted for epilepsy and prescribed medication, refused flat out to sign off on the death certificate. Didn't want to put his name to it. Dan was surprised too when he heard about the conclusion. He had thought Ted's condition was serious, but he didn't know it could be fatal.

Dan left Ted's place and went looking for the cats, rounded them up and left them with a cat-loving neighbour (the estate manager was threatening to have them put down if he found them–"You can't do that," Dan said. "They're Ted's!"). Then he went to stay at his then girlfriend's house. And never heard from the police again. He felt bad that something had happened to Ted on his watch and he had been unable to save him. He couldn't help wondering if he could or should have done more. He went to the memorial service fully expecting to be quizzed. But nothing, just the paddle-out. He had an address and a phone number and he assumed that in the end somebody would come and knock on his door or at least call. Whether it was the police or someone else. But nada. No follow-up. Investigation closed. Nobody asking questions.

"Not until you turned up," he said.

He knew a lot. More than he really wanted to say, I had the impression. Omertà was normal on the North Shore.

Nobody wanted to get into trouble, everybody wanted a quiet time. Including the police.

Which may seem like a strange thing to say. But, isn't this their job precisely, you may say? Isn't this what happens in the movies? The bad guys do bad things and then the cops turn up and solve the crime and the bad guys go down or are taken down. Sounds simple enough, but in reality things are much more complicated. There are compromises. You can't achieve purity and righteousness and the kingdom of god, least of all on the North Shore. For one thing, the police in Honolulu had always thought of the North Shore as Hawaii's Wild West. What happened on the North Shore stayed on the North Shore. So long as it didn't impinge on the rest of the island. Country was country, as Ted had pointed out. It was not Town. Town was the realm of the law (even if perpetually transgressed). Country was lawless. A place of outlaws. And, if you think about it, police officers have to live there too, in Hawaii. They don't live in fortresses. They all have families. They want a quiet life. What was the point in poking a stick in a nest of vipers? You were only going to stir things up. As the report states, there were "no signs of any foul play." Even though, according to Dan, the signs of it were all over the place. Did Hawaii need another murder? It would be bad for tourism, for one thing. Just imagine all those tabloid headlines: "English Lord Slain On Oahu." It would help no one, and as for Ted himself, well, he was already dead, so he wasn't going to say much about it. Ted died on October 4, 1997; the case was "closed" and laid to rest on November 24, 1997. By which time Ted had already been cremated and his ashes dissolved forever into the deep blue Pacific ocean.

Prior to the cremation, Ted's stepmother Rachel recalls, the funeral director told her not to look at the body. "It's not a pretty sight," he said. Beyond his powers to prettify.

I can't agree that Ted had "no enemies." He had at least one well-known enemy. Possibly more than one. One woman I interviewed reckoned that her husband had had a hand in it (and he had done time for other offences). And Ted had already received a warning, delivered by two heavy guys "in suits." Potential assailants were queuing up. What would be the next step? The correct next step would be for Ted to stay away from Lola, as he had agreed. But of course, as we know, he had not been able to stay away from Lola. He was obsessed with Lola, how could he keep away? She was the perfect woman, after all. But he had thereby disrespected *the management*. So he would have to pay for that. He would have to be sanctioned. You couldn't just let him get away with that. Lord or no lord. But you wouldn't kill him, would you? No. The next step would be to rough him up a little. Just a gentle reminder. But maybe the guys wouldn't be quite so polite this time around. Maybe this time they would cross the threshold. Maybe Ted would even invite them in. And then they would have to teach him a lesson. It was strictly business, nothing personal, he just had to learn to stay away from Lola, once and for all. Maybe, just maybe, they would shove him in the bath, for good measure, after they had knocked him around. And maybe, when they heard later that he had died, they would express a measure of surprise, even regret: they hadn't meant to kill him, that wasn't part of it. They were only supposed to "slap" him. The death was an unfortunate accident. But it was too late now.

I don't know any of this. It's just what a few reasonable people think may have happened. It's only a hypothesis. No more probable or improbable than the "natural causes" in the police report. But when I mentioned this theory to his ex-wife Susan in Brisbane, she could see it happening in just this way. She knew that Ted would not readily give up Lola. "He was like that," she said. "If someone told him not to do something, and he thought that was wrong, he would want to do it for sure." As if someone had thrown down the gauntlet and he was honour-bound to pick it up.

And then she said something which has stayed with me and I can still hear her saying it right now, as if I was still at Montezuma's Mexican restaurant in a suburb of Brisbane and I was listening to her as she sits across the table from me and a look of recognition comes over her.

"Then he will have known true love for the first time," she said. By "then" she meant, at the very moment at which he was dying. "He never really knew true love until that point." The point of death. The Charge of the Light Brigade. Our own Shangri-La. Valhalla.

In the Excalibur program, Ted had written: "The future looks bright for the healthy, exciting and glamorous sport of professional surfing." But there was no more future, not for Ted.

Few of us get to die for a reason. Had Ted drowned surfing Sunset, the way Rabbit thought he had died, then he would have died for no reason, or rather died in exchange for the pleasure that surfing afforded him. But at the point at which he ended up in the bath with his legs sticking out at the side and he felt the life force fleeing from him, receding like a tide, he might have thought (and this was what Susan, who had been closest to him, was thinking) that at least he was dying for something. For someone. He was dying for Lola. He was dying for love. "That should be the ultimate goal of everyone," Susan said.

In death Ted had finally become the hero he always wanted to be. "Killed in action."

42.

Sunset Beach is like Piccadilly Circus—eventually, everyone passes through. Movie stars (G. Clooney), painters (D. Hockney, in his trademark white cap), and Randy Rarick. Well, Randy Rarick lives right there. He roams around the world, but he always goes back.

It was the 30th anniversary of the World Cup of Surfing, sponsored by O'Neill, a few winters after the death of Ted, when I bumped into Randy outside the contest trailer. There were the usual tumbling turquoise walls of water ten feet high and the usual men in shorts spraying their personal signatures across them like demented graffiti artists. The waves, ascending out of the ocean like sea monsters, furiously set about erasing all this incomprehensible calligraphy. Miraculously spat out of the barrel in a fury of foam and thunder, surfers were waving their arms overhead like extremely tanned muscular evangelicals, assured of an afterlife.

While we were talking about this and that, Randy and I, another Japanese tourist bus pulled in and a few dozen highly disciplined tourists trooped out, took a few pictures and trooped back in again. Followed by an obscenely stretched white limo. Whose passengers didn't even bother to get out, preferring to spectate in air-conditioned elongated splendour.

"I live here and I look at what I've done," Rarick said in a lazy drawling mea culpa. "We've hit saturation point." He felt that there was an inevitability to it–the slow and painful slide of paradise into a kind of hell. Once upon a time Waimea Bay, the holy of holies, a few miles to the south of Sunset, was seen as too big, beyond merely human powers; then it was pioneered by a handful of big-wave heroes; and now when Waimea has a big swell there were–on the last count–eighty-five guys out there: eighty-five guys going for one wave. Like a traffic jam on water. Waimea Bay has become the M25 of surfing. The Few, like old spitfire pilots, have been displaced by a Jumbo-load of passengers. They wanted to make surfing sexy. Maybe they made it too sexy. The result was bound to be a population explosion. O'Neill–and other beachwear companies–were sponsoring kids as young as eight. By the age of twelve young pretenders to the Triple Crown were already gearing up for or shadowing the pro tour. No wonder the North Shore had hit overload. Ted was a victim of the Malthusian principle.

On this day Andy Irons (shortly before he died from substance abuse–or substances in his case) was jousting with Kelly Slater. Then I got tangled up in an episode of *North Shore*. A surfside soap opera from Fox TV. "This is NOT *Baywatch*," said Nathaniel (whose job appeared to be to shout out "rolling"). I assumed this was Hollywood speak for "this IS *Baywatch*." Or something very like it. "It has some real serious drama." It was true. A handsome hunk, called Gabriel, was canoodling down on the water's edge with Jade. They both looked as if they were grown in vats. Every now and then a team of technicians swarmed around them and doused them in extra fake tan and gave them some kind of emergency cosmetic surgery. Jade stormed off in a bikini-clad huff because Gabriel revealed that he loves another–the ocean– and always will, or something like that. It was something Ted had already felt, from *Storm Riders*, through *Asian Paradise* and beyond, that surfing has become almost indistinguishable from celluloid. Hip has coalesced with hype. If you're not on YouTube then you don't exist.

Martin Potter–Britain's one and only world champion, in 1989–wandered by. He was retired, a kind of elder statesman figure, the surfing republic's ambassador to the United Nations or equivalent: a commentator on the young guns. There was one forty-year-old competing–Ted's age when he died–Tom Curren. Former world champion, still stylish, not quite a punch-drunk old boxer getting back in the ring, but completely outgunned by the new kids on the block. "I was just unprepared," he protested, to anyone who would listen.

I said to Randy something about how I used to think old surfers rode off over the horizon, like Shane, or found a berth in Valhalla's hall of heroes. "Do you want to know where Glen Winton is now?" said Randy. In his heyday, Winton was known as Mr X and he carved the straightest lines on the biggest waves and he looked the Minotaur square in the eye. "He is a doorman somewhere in northern New South Wales." He could have been a contender; and now he's a bouncer. It felt a little like twilight of the idols.

I gazed out at all those perfect waves. "I was thinking Ted should have been here," I said. "This swell is just right for him."

"Ted was lucky," Randy said.

43.

In 2017, twenty years after the death of Ted, I went to see Bernie Baker, who lived just across the Kam Highway from Sunset. He still had one of Ted's boards. A twin-fin, sub-six feet, round tail. It had been shaped by Mark Richards back in May 1984. I took it out at Haleiwa on a small day, to get the feel of it. As I paddled out I was acutely aware that I had a sword right in front of my nose. Excalibur was spraygunned onto the board. It felt like the whole board was a sword and I was wielding it. I pointed it at the horizon, in the direction of Asia. I swung around and pointed it at the green mountains of Oahu. I had the feeling I could do anything. On this board I could not just ride a wave, I could go out and conquer the whole world or track down the Holy Grail.

"Great board!" said a guy. I had leaned the board against a palm tree while I was towelling down. The guy had a bushy grey beard, but he was fit and sinewy. T-shirt, shorts, sandals, standard dress.

"It's a bit historic," I said.

He came closer and scrutinized. "M-R. Mark Richards! He could really surf. They don't surf like that any more."

"No," I said.

"What's with the sword?"

"Excalibur," I said.

"Not Lord Ted?"

"You knew him?"

Turned out that the guy was a sailor. Not exactly an ancient mariner but close. Spent half the year in New Zealand, half in Alaska. Was on his way up to Alaska now. His boat was moored in the harbor. He was going to sail on but the unusual summer swell had detained him. He'd arrived in March, picked up some huge waves, and then stuck around. He promised he would finally get going next week. People would start to think in terms of icebergs and such.

"I saw him surf," he said.

"When was this?"

"A while ago. Does it matter?"

"No," I said.

"It was a winter anyhow. He had this way of leaning forwards. Like, I don't know, the figurehead on the front of a ship. Like he was at an angle to the rest of the universe. Like he should have fallen off. But he didn't."

"Where was this?"

The guy looked back in time in his head. He hadn't forgotten a moment of it. "Sunset. I surfed bigger waves back then. But it was huge. So I stayed out on the shoulder. There were a few guys who were standing right up in the tube. Ted was one of them. Three or four seconds, really solid tubes. Just kept going on. Wave after wave, set after set. It was one of those days. Endless."

For a moment, I felt like Duncan Coventry, I had the sense that Ted really was there, still surfing, for ever and ever, at Sunset or Waimea or Pipeline, and at the same time perched on my shoulder, like a pirate's parrot and whispering in my ear, just as he had written to Deya': "I'd probably make the same mistikes if I did it all over again."

ACKNOWLEDGEMENTS

Over the ages, I've missed out on a lot of good waves. And I'll miss plenty more. Similarly, I'm about to miss out – reluctantly or accidentally – some very important people. But I definitely couldn't have written this book without the generous thoughts and insights of the following: Tony Alva, Bernie Baker, Mike Baker, Tim Barrow, Rabbit Bartholomew, Paul Blacker, Deya' Bradic, Steph Broadribb, John Callahan, Duncan Coventry, Rachel Coventry, Richard Cram, Dan, Phil Holden, Paul Holmes, Dick Hoole, Greg Huglin, Carmel Hunter, Derek Hynd, Carolyn Jones, Pete Jones, Susan Knight, Heather Martin, Linda Nash, Randy Rarick, Peter Scott, Heather Thomas, Shaun Tomson, Pete Townend, Matt Warshaw, Alex Williams.

Alongside teaching French at Cambridge University and writing a column for the *Independent* newspaper in the UK, Andy Martin has travelled the world as a keen surfer. He got to know Ted Deerhurst when reporting on the international circuit as surfing correspondent for the *Times* of London. He is the author of numerous books including: *With Child, Reacher Said Nothing, The Boxer and the Goalkeeper: Sartre vs Camus, Stealing the Wave* and *Walking on Water*.